'The seven French Dominicans whose stories come alive in this volume had a profound impact on the renewal of Catholic theology in the twentieth century and helped to usher in the Second Vatican Council. Thanks to Thomas O'Meara and Paul Philibert, these prophetic voices echo in our day and have the power to inspire equally creative forms of witness to the Gospel in the twenty-first century.'

Mary Catherine Hilkert, O.P.
Professor of Theology
University of Notre Dame, U.S.A.

'Fifty years after Vatican II it is still far too common to find interpretations of the council's teaching that are innocent of its larger historical context. This book, written by two esteemed theologians, goes far in correcting this failing. The authors remind us that the French Dominicans of the early twentieth century, in ways great and small, played a role in raising key themes that would be developed by the council. Each of the seven Dominicans whose work is discussed quite accessibly in this brief volume helped nudge Catholicism toward a more vital, dynamic, and dialogical vision of the church. Their contributions merit our attention and our gratitude.'

Richard R. Gaillardetz
McCarthy Professor of Catholic Systermatic Theology
Boston College, U.S.A.

'This is a deeply refreshing book about seven Dominican brethren who fearlessly brought their faith into dialogue with different aspects of modernity. It captures their joy, freedom, courage, and their profound evangelical hope in the face of fear and hostility. I could not put it down. I knew and lived with many of the Dominicans mentioned in this book. It captures them perfectly.'

Timothy Radcliffe, O.P.
Former Dominican Master General
Author of *Take the Plunge: Living Baptism and Confirmation*

D1712979

Dominican Series

The Dominican Series is a joint project by Australian Dominican women and men and offers contributions on topics of Dominican interest and various aspects of church, theology and religion in the world.

Series Editors: Mark O'Brien OP and Gabrielle Kelly OP

1. *English for Theology: A Resource for Teachers and Students*,
   Gabrielle Kelly OP, 2004.

2. *Towards the Intelligent Use of Liberty: Dominican Approaches in Education*,
   edited by Gabrielle Kelly OP and Kevin Saunders OP, 2007.

3. *Preaching Justice: Dominican Contributions to Social Ethics in the Twentieth Century*,
   edited by Francesco Campagnoni OP and Helen Alford OP, 2008.

4. *Don't Put Out The Burning Bush: Worship and preaching in a Complex World*,
   edited by Vivian Boland, 2008.

5. *Bible Dictionary: Selected Biblical and Theological Words*,
   Gabrielle Kelly OP in collaboration with Joy Sandefur, 2008.

6. *Sunday Matters A: Reflections on the Lectionary Readings for Year A*,
   Mark O'Brien OP, 2010.

7. *Sunday Matters B: Reflections on the Lectionary Readings for Year B*,
   Mark O'Brien OP, 2011.

8. *Sunday Matters C: Reflections on the Lectionary Readings for Year C*,
   Mark O'Brien OP, 2012.

SCANNING
THE SIGNS OF THE TIMES

FRENCH DOMINICANS IN THE
TWENTIETH CENTURY

Thomas F O'Meara
Paul Philibert

ATF Theology
Adelaide

2013

Front and back covers (photos of La Tourette): © François Diot, 2010.

Cover design by Astrid Sengkey
Layout/Artwork by Anna Dimasi

Text Minion Pro Size 11

Published by:

An imprint of the ATF Ltd.
PO Box 504
Hindmarsh, SA 5007
ABN 90 116 359 963
www.atfpress.com

*Dedicated to the Dominican Friars from around the world
who contributed to Vatican II*

Le Saulchoir
Étiolles (France)

Our Seven 20th Century French Dominicans

Antonin-Gilbert Sertillanges

M-D Chenu

Yves Congar

Louis-Joseph Lebret

Jacques Loew

Pierre-André Liégé

Marie-Alain Couturier

CONTENTS

Le Saulchoir
Kain-les-Tournai (Belgium)

French Dominicans in the Twentieth Century

This book focuses on some key figures of the Catholic Church in France in modern times. There, in the course of the twentieth century, theologians and pastors passed from an attitude of comfortable entitlement or cultural isolation to a new attitude of apostolic creativity. Similar changes took place elsewhere in Europe, but not with the same intensity. These stories of the French church provide crucial background for understanding the Ecumenical Council Vatican II. The council brought about a renewal in practice and perspective since the 1960s that has changed the life of the Catholic Church. The renewal of theology and worship, the event of the council, and the church's new presence in society continue to have important repercussions today.

What happened in France and why was it so important? These seven Dominicans were prophetically able to read the signs of the times, as Vatican II's Constitution on the Church in the Modern World puts it. They saw what the Holy Spirit was doing in the church and the world around them and found ways to address the challenges pastorally. That this occurred in France, a traditionally Catholic nation that became a cradle of pastoral innovation, is significant.

For centuries, the French Catholic Church considered itself to be the church's 'eldest daughter' or the oldest Christian nation. This idea was linked to the baptism of Clovis I, King of the Franks, at Rheims in 479 by St. Remigius. That early event became the ideological buttress for centuries of absolute monarchy. France, with its 'three estates' of clergy, nobility, and common people, represented a Christian ideal of hierarchical order where everyone had 'his' place. Over time this rigid structure became the source of resentment and division. After the Protestant Reformation, France became divided by Calvinism religiously and politically. (In the seventeenth century, about ten percent of the French became Protestant.) This resulted in political strife between provinces and in bloody religious wars. It also encouraged the throne's cynical abuse of power to enable it to control religious and political life. In reaction, the Enlightenment proposed a new ideal of human equality and eventually led France into the Revolution of 1789 that repudiated religion, reacting to the church's long toleration of abuses by the monarchy.

That was the context in the middle of the nineteenth century for the life of Henri Dominique Lacordaire. A native of the area of Dijon, after a period of agnosticism in his teens, he regained his Catholic faith as a young lawyer in Paris. Soon his dream was to reconcile the church with the revolutionary ideals of 'freedom, equality, and fraternity'. Considered the greatest pulpit preacher of the nineteenth century, Lacordaire decided to become a Dominican and to reintroduce the Order of Preachers to his homeland. His charge to his young followers was 'God and Liberty!' His eloquence and popularity were remarkable, and in the 1840s Lacordaire began reopening Dominican priories in Nancy, Paris, Toulouse and other cities. Especially attracted by the Dominican constitutions, which are thoroughly democratic, Lacordaire saw the Order both as a workshop for demonstrating that democratic principles can enrich the Christian life and as a work force to reconcile the church's theology and preaching with a new age and its ideas. Lacordaire influenced all the figures presented in our study.

Lacordaire was a fearless proponent of spiritual freedom in an authoritarian church and a defender of the church in an anticlerical society. He had the gift of going to the heart of disputed questions and lucidly persuading people to understand the church's rights and its contribution to a true humanism. The French Dominicans' courage and optimism mirror Lacordaire and his heritage. If there is a 'spirit' or *esprit* of the French Dominican intellectuals of the twentieth century, it comes in great part from Lacordaire.

Each of the seven Dominicans sketched in our book visualised the church as a community awakening to a vital and inclusive life. Each also had to overcome the resistance of ecclesiastical authorities who were complacent with privilege and custom. These Dominicans imagined the church as responsible for the present and the future and not just as a museum of the past. Whereas Lacordaire was reacting to the aftereffects of the French Revolution, these seven Dominicans were contending with the

Holy See's reactionary fear of modernity in the early twentieth century. In spite of obstacles from ecclesiastical and political leaders, they persevered to realise their vision. They were scanning the signs of the times in pastoral life, the economy, social change, and the arts. In doing so, they sketched new possibilities for the future.

All through the nineteenth century, the popes and their central administration found it impossible to conceive of the church without the ancient structures of monarchy and feudalism. Popular democracy was an aberration and a threat to hierarchy. New methods of historical research and information discovered by the social sciences were considered dangerous to the established privileges of the hierarchical order. Nonetheless, thoughtful Catholics everywhere were wondering how they might work to emerge from such an iron cage of ecclesiastical decrepitude. They wanted to step out into modern society and demonstrate the church's virtues as a model community. Christian community formed the background for the theological work and pastoral creativity of the men described in the following chapters.

How to break out? As a philosopher and preacher, Antonin-Gilbert Sertillanges recognised that one way out was to insist that the church was not a uniform Roman corporation, but a community of faithful nations, each with its own characteristic genius. He was a philosopher, but also a public intellectual much in the style of Lacordaire. Then, Marie-Dominique Chenu, as an historian and mentor of church leaders, discovered that the theology of Aquinas was not, as supposed, a fixed and changeless compilation of philosophical and religious axioms, but a brilliant reading of ancient sources in the light of living questions. As a prophet and theologian of the church, Yves Congar meticulously reconstructed the components of a theology that sees the church as a living organism, reuniting Scriptures and pastoral life in a persuasive way. As an economist and a moral theologian, Louis-Joseph Lebret observed the needs and the potential of Catholics who were alienated both spiritually and socially. Lebret was one of the first great artisans of social planning aimed at just and self-sustaining societies. Pierre-André Liégé recognised the mighty force that a catechetical awakening of the laity represents, and he became the architect of programs for adult faith formation for people at work in the world and of new approaches for pastors and catechists. Jacques Loew, as a priest-worker and spiritual director, found ways to express the holiness of the spiritual life embedded in the workplace, the family, the factory, and the neighborhood. As a theologian of the arts, Marie-Alain Couturier recognised that beauty should be incarnated in forms that call people beyond religious sentimentality into a wide-awake awareness of the real world and of God's presence there.

These seven theologians shared a common mission to bring about a renewal in the life of the church, one that would touch not just priests and bishops but all the baptised. They helped to recapture the spirit of evangelization that represents the church's vocation through the centuries. Their stories illuminate in different ways the age-old tension between nostalgia and hope, faintheartedness and courage. Their projects survived through the twentieth century and on into our own century. Their fundamental questions remain ours as well: the nature of the church, the vocation of the baptised, the presence of grace in the world, and the power of the Holy Spirit reverberating in society and culture. Their lives and activities are rooted in the history of their period, but they transcend that past to be a forceful influence for the church today.

* * *

This book is the collaboration of Thomas O'Meara and Paul Philibert who together wrote this introduction and also the conclusion, entitled 'The Church in History'. Thomas O'Meara wrote chapters one, three, five and seven. Paul Philibert wrote chapters two, four and six.

* * *

Acknowledgements

We are grateful to Jean-Pierre Jossua for writing the Preface of this book and setting the scene for what unfolds here. He is an influential Dominican writer residing in Paris who lived for many years with several of these figures and who was Congar's biographer. We likewise thank another Paris Dominican, Michel Albaric, archivist of the Province of France, for his generous assistance, particularly for finding the photographs used here and making them available to us. The late Antoine Lion of the Priory of Saint-Jacques, long interested in M-A Couturier, provided the photograph of Couturier. We are grateful to Myriam Frebet and to Cecilia Wilkinson Enns for reading some of the chapters and providing useful criticism and suggestions, and to John Philibert for digitally editing the photographs.

Preface:

A Remarkable Evolution

Profiting from favorable circumstances that included a large number of new recruits following the war of 1914–1918 and the presence of several truly remarkable personalities, the Dominican Provinces of France (Paris) and Lyons reached unprecedented heights during the years 1930 to 1970, an achievement probably not to be equaled again. The Province of Toulouse, whose spirit was different from the beginning, developed in its own way during that time. Père Henri-Dominique Lacordaire was the start of it all. He refounded the Order of Preachers in France in the middle of the nineteenth century, giving it a spirit that was distinct from how the Order appeared elsewhere at that time.

The Order in France was sympathetic to its own time and yearned to engage its contemporaries' interest in proclaiming the gospel. It had a great spirit of freedom and was eager to prepare its members to be intellectually serious. This spirit fed into many kinds of initiatives. For example, there was the social apostolate beginning at the start of the twentieth century with Vincent Maumus and later the work of Louis-Joseph Lebret and Thomas Suavet at *Économie et Humanisme*; cultural initiatives with journals like the *Revue des Jeunes* of Matthieu Barge, and then *La Vie Intellectuelle* and *Signes du Temps*. There were apostolic initiatives to take on new Dominican foundations in Scandinavia, in Vietnam, and in Africa, as well as involvement with the priest-workers after the war of 1940-1945; publishing ventures with the Éditions du Cerf and a variety of magazines such as *Lumière et Vie* in Lyons; and finally ecumenical endeavors through the centers *Istina* in Paris and *Saint-Irénée* in Lyons.

Special attention should be given to formation in the intellectual life within the Province of France. This point is important not only because of the outstanding results it produced but because it gave life to the many initiatives just mentioned and sustained their influence. To explain this point well I have to tell succinctly the story of the house of studies that will be called Le Saulchoir at the beginning of the twentieth century.

Although it was expelled from France at the time of the exile of religious orders in 1904, the Province's studium had taken a very consequential step in 1881. In that year Père Réginald Baudoin became the Regent of Studies and established the practice of *a return to the original texts* during a period of great mediocrity in ecclesiastical studies when theology was being taught everywhere from manuals. In 1894, Ambroise Gardeil took charge of the college and insisted that the studium needed to achieve a *level of studies in theology worthy of a university*, including teaching those *scientific disciplines*, both religious and secular, that are indispensible for theology's scientific development. In 1893, Gardeil was a co-founder of a first French Dominican theological journal, the *Revue Thomiste*, published first in Fribourg, Switzerland, then in Toulouse, France. In 1905, the studium moved to Kain in Belgium, to a place known as Le Saulchoir, meaning the willow grove.

Le Saulchoir was founded there and would play a role in the renewal of Thomistic studies following Leo XIII's initiatives and would become involved in the controversies emerging from the church's first confrontation with 'modernity' in the intellectual life. The Dominican theologians made themselves known as a solid front in important ways, and yet they still remained rather closed on a number of questions that would not go away. At the same time a historical consciousness was developing among the Dominicans with the foundation in 1892 of the *Revue Biblique* at the École Biblique in Jerusalem by Marie-Joseph Lagrange (of the Toulouse province) and with the historical work of Pierre Mandonnet in Fribourg. In 1907, at the initiative of Père Mannès Jacquin, a second theological journal belonging to Le Saulchoir was founded with the title the *Revue des Sciences Philosophiques et Théologiques*. (It has recently celebrated its hundredth anniversary).

Following the dispersal of friars who went off to the First World War and then with an influx of new members continuing in the 1920s, studies at Le Saulchoir underwent a further revival, taking a decidedly historical character. This was due to the influence of the Regent of Studies after 1911, Père Antoine Lemonnyer (who was a disciple of both Lagrange and Gardeil), as well as thanks to the eventual arrival of Mandonnet at Le Saulchoir. At that time the field of medieval studies began to develop there, and the application of historical method to the study of St Thomas Aquinas became a characteristic trait of the school. An institute of medieval studies was founded at Le Saulchoir in collaboration with Étienne Gilson who had introduced medieval studies at the Sorbonne, and these enterprises would lead to a similar foundation in Canada.

In 1934, while still located at Kain in Belgium, the two pontifical faculties of theology and philosophy of Le Saulchoir were canonically erected. Le Saulchoir numbered twenty-two professors and one hundred twenty students (including non-Dominicans). Soon Le Saulchoir would be transferred to a town in France called Étiolles, not far from Paris. In the 1920s and later, studies in philosophy also developed at Le Saulchoir, with an openness to the philosophy of Kant; they were marked by the the work of M-D Roland-Gosselin, and later of A-D Festugière and Dominique Dubarle. Here is where the activity of Père Dalmace Sertillanges fits in; even though not conducted at Le Saulchoir, his work is important, well known in America, and studied in this book.

In 1932, Marie-Dominique Chenu became Regent of Studies, and along with his friends Henri-Marie Féret and Yves M-J Congar, he would give Le Saulchoir an international reputation. Chenu was present at Le Saulchoir in Kain from 1920 onwards. He was a friar gifted with a marvelous human spirit and a spark of genius. His preoccupation to get to the bottom of the Christian faith was linked to his concern to maintain a university level of studies, a rigorous methodology (especially through historical study), and openness to the real issues of the church and of society. For Chenu, true history uses the present as a source of renewal to understand the fertile contributions of the tradition. Knowledge of the past illumines the most advanced new research. You will find in this book a competent study of these very issues.

The second theme that I want to consider here is paying serious attention to the real world. This focus arose especially from what happened in Paris following the Second World War and it expressed the Dominicans' great confidence in society's movement toward freedom and human dignity. Are freedom and dignity too much to hope for? Regardless, between the time of Chenu's activities at Le Saulchoir at Étiolles and his activities with the Dominicans in Paris, there were two momentous disruptions: the first was due to World War II, and the second was due to the destructive consequences for Le Saulchoir of Rome's negative judgment upon Chenu's manifesto, *Une École de Théologie: Le Saulchoir*. Put on the *Index of For-*

bidden Books, Chenu's work became the emblem of a crisis arising from the Roman authorities' mistrust of history, from the resentment of the authors of the theological manuals, and from the ambitions of another group of Dominicans. Père Chenu was exiled from Le Saulchoir to Paris.

Chenu's fostering of the evolution of the intellectual and apostolic mission of his province, along with the work of his friends, was prominent both before and after the war. Examples of this influence are the publications of Éditions du Cerf under the guidance of Pierre Boisselot and Augustin Maydieu, the involvement of friars in the apostolic initiatives of the priest-workers, and the efforts of other remarkable personalities like Pierre-André Liégé, who was called 'the pillar of catechesis' by a Portuguese cardinal not known for exaggeration.

After the crisis of 1942, Le Saulchoir became divided between new professors with a 'speculative' and 'spiritual' tendency, and the others who held for the historical method. At times there were issues of aloofness and suspicion among them, and also the tension between a glorious image of the school and its present reality. However, there were positive elements too, especially after 1945. Again there was a large influx of new friars following the war. Senior professors like Hyacinthe Dondaine in theology and L-B Geiger in philosophy handed on the school's values. A generation of new professors began to teach, and the first signs of the renewal of biblical, patristic, liturgical, and ecumenical theologies were beginning to be felt. By 1956, Le Saulchoir had recaptured its rigorous intellectual and religious life—although due to some teachers' pedagogical limitations often only the most gifted really profited from its program. A hundred students led a beautiful community life, while the 'lectors', the teachers, stayed apart.

The publication of the theological journal *Revue des Sciences Philosophiques et Théologiques* was resumed. The Leonine Commission, responsible for the critical edition of the works of St Thomas Aquinas, was located at Étiolles. In the last years of this period, down to 1968, under Claude Geffré as Regent of Studies, a second generation of new professors, working together, began teaching at Le Saulchoir and they shared an openness to modern philosophy, religious studies, and the fields of social science and psychology. I must add to this narrative a particularly important presence.

Yves Congar, after an absence due to the war and his captivity, was present at Étiolles from 1945 to 1954 (the year of a new crisis concerning theologians suspected of 'progressive tendencies' and complicity in the priest-worker movement), and he pursued research that would become an essential contribution of Le Saulchoir to the preparation of Vatican II. After his various exiles that started in 1954 and that included a long stay in Strasbourg, Congar returned to Le Saulchoir in 1967.

A few more words about Congar will indicate his place in the story of Le Saulchoir and his contribution to the life of his Province. (You will find in this book a chapter on Congar that dispenses me from saying more.) He was born in a Catholic milieu in the Ardennes and was trained at the diocesan seminary in Paris called 'Les Carmes', where he came under the influence of Jacques Maritain who was, however, closely linked to the Thomistic tendencies of the Toulouse Dominican Province which were more ahistorical and speculative. Jacques Loew, an engaging apostolic leader who was the product of Toulouse, recognised the limits of that perspective in his later years (according to the biography written by Georges Convert).

In 1926, arriving at Le Saulchoir, Yves Congar discovered history. For him, the historian's work provides an understanding of what is real and allows scholars to direct a particular historical situation back to a deeper tradition. Congar surprised his teachers when in 1930 he decided to dedicate his life to the work of Christian unity. He thought of this not as a specialization but rather as a charism, a dimension of everything Christian, drawn from friendships and contacts with real living people. Ecumenism is inseparable from a renewal in ecclesiology, a theology of the church that understands the church as mystery and as communion. In 1937, Père Congar created the collection *Unam Sanctam* and published his *Chrétiens désunis: principes d'un oecuménisme catholique* (*Divided Christendom: A Catholic Study of the Problems of Reunion*). Pushed out of ecumenical work following the war and aware of the volatile spirit of those times, he nonetheless wrote great works that would assist the development of Vatican II. Along with other theologians, Congar would play an essential role at the council. Even until his death, his thinking about ecclesiology and about ecumenism continued to develop with greater and greater openness.

This is not the place to describe the final period of Le Saulchoir, from 1968 to 1974. First at Étiolles and then in Paris, Congar continued to encourage and sustain others with his friendship. There was a rather successful revision of the Le Saulchoir study program in 1968, but the faculties of philosophy and theology were closed down in 1974 because of an insufficient number of students. The basic studies of the Dominican friars of the Province of France were transferred to another faculty at the end of the 1970s. Today, there are still a number of institutions close to the Priory of Saint-Jacques in Paris that continue the work of Le Saulchoir and that work in close collaboration. These include the ecumenical center *Istina*, the Leonine Commission, the Provincial Archives, the Library of Le Saulchoir, the *Revue des Sciences Philosophiques et Théologiques,* and most recently, Éditions du Cerf. As a Center of Studies, Le Saulchoir presents brief courses and seminars.

The great adventure has come to an end. It bore its fruit, and some of those results still endure.

Jean-Pierre Jossua

Chapter 1

Antonin-Gilbert Sertillanges:
Between Christian Belief and Modern Culture

Antonin-Gilbert Sertillanges belongs to the generation prior to that of prominent Dominicans like M-D Chenu and Yves Congar. His efforts provided the initiative, the orientation and key impetus for the varied Dominican theological and pastoral renewals that developed in the twentieth century. He was a remarkable personality who could think creatively about medieval theology and modern ethics, art and society.

Sertillanges was born on November 17, 1863, in Clermont-Ferrand. Hours in the classrooms of the Brothers of the Christian Schools found expansion in walks through the picturesque city with its remnants of a medieval Dominican priory. Past memories of Blaise Pascal drew his creative and romantic spirit toward faith and religion. 'I worked, certainly . . . but in a different way. When mathematics was the subject, I thought about poetry; when poetry was the subject, I wondered about mathematics.'[1] The preaching of M-J Ollivier, OP, inspired his decision to take the path he had been considering: to enter religious life, to enter the Dominicans. Ollivier (1835–1910) was a powerful preacher whose themes were the proclamation of God's actions in the world and the application of Jesus' life to current affairs.[2] At the Cathedral of Notre Dame in Paris, he preached a series of sermons on the purpose and nature of the church subsequently published as *L'Eglise, Sa Raison d'Être,*[3] a book anticipating somewhat the future enterprises of his young hearer.

---

1. M-F Moos, 'Preface', A-D Sertillanges, *L'Univers et l'âme* (Paris: Les Éditions Ouvrières, 1965), 8.
2. André Duval, 'Ollivier, François, Jean-Marie [Marie-Joseph]', in *Dictionnaire de spiritualité* 11 (Paris: Beauchesne, 1982), 185f.
3. (Paris: Lethielleux, 1897).

Sertillanges entered the Dominican Province of France on September 8, 1883, receiving the religious name of Antonin-Gilbert. Buildings at Belmonte, Spain, loaned by French nobility, allowed the Dominicans to establish a novitiate after the expulsion of religious orders from France in 1880. He studied theology at Corbara in Corsica, another outpost of the exiled friars, and after his ordination in 1888 he taught in that house of studies and then in Amiens. Assigned to Paris in 1893, he went to Italy for several weeks where art inspired his first book, a dialogue between religion and painting in Tuscany, *Un Pélérinage Artistique à Florence* published in 1896.[4] That perspective lasted throughout his life: faith and art expressing themselves in certain ages through similar themes and forms. Art and theology illustrated each other, for instance, in a Romanesque or Gothic style. Over the years, in several sets of lectures on Christianity, he used pictures of masterpieces to explain the themes of faith.[5]

Sertillanges became professor of moral theology at the Institut Catholique of Paris, holding that position from 1900 to 1920. He concentrated on deepening his knowledge of Thomas Aquinas and on gaining knowledge about contemporary philosophy in the university world. His study of Immanuel Kant soon yielded to encounters with contemporary French thinkers, particularly with the dynamic theories of Henri Bergson.[6]

---

4.   (Paris: Lecoffre, 1903; reprinted in 1931). See M Pradines, *Notice sur la vie et les oeuvres du R. P. Antonin Sertillanges* (Paris: Institut de France, 1951); M-F Moos, 'Un Maître de la vie spirituelle: le T. R. P. Sertillanges, O.P.', in *La Vie spirituelle* 80 (1949): 607–33; F de Urmenela, 'Caracteristicas del Tomismo según Grabmann y Sertillanges', in *La Ciencia Tomista* 77 (1950): 227–35; Moos, *Le Père Sertillanges, maître de la vie spirituelle* (Bruxelles: La Pensée Catholique, 1957); A Piolanti, 'P. Antonin Dalmace Sertillanges, O.P.: Un tomista da non dimenticare', in *Doctor communis* 41 (1988): 79–90; MH Vicaire, 'Sertillanges, Antonin Gilbert', in *New Catholic Encyclopedia* 13 (Washington: McGraw-Hill, 1967): 125f; André Duval, 'Sertillanges (Antonin Gilbert)', in *Dictionnaire de spiritualité* 15 (Paris: Beauchesne, 1988), 668–71; Franz-Martin Schmölz, 'Antonin-Dalmace Sertillanges (1863–1948)', in Emil Coreth *et al*, *Christliche Philosophie im katholischen Denken des 19. und 20. Jahrhunderts* 2 (Graz: Styria, 1988), 485–92.
5.   Moos, 'Préface', 13.
6.   'The death of Henri Bergson has been a loss for the world; it is equally—this should surprise no one—a loss for Catholicism. Mystical souls recognise that God is great to an infinite degree . . . In terms of Catholicism the position of Bergson, as his books present it to us, is not an adherence. He was a philosopher . . . but he was—I can bear witness to this—fully persuaded of the legitimacy of faith' (Sertillanges, *Henri Bergson et le catholicisme* [Paris: Flammarion, 1941], 5–7; this book was translated into Japanese in 1977). At the end of his life Bergson was thinking about Christ as a summit and Christ as a man. For Bergson the church is 'Christ socialized' where the individual

His two volumes on Thomas Aquinas appearing in 1910 were followed by *La Philosophie Morale de S. Thomas d'Aquin* in 1916.[7] He published a number of books on apologetics. One of these, *Les Sources de la Croyance en Dieu,* published in 1903 had twenty-two editions, and an early edition stated that over 10,000 copies were already in print.

During the persecution of church organisations in 1903, Sertillanges organised measures to sustain Catholic intellectual life in Paris. In 1915, he took over the influential journal of theology and religious cultural criticism, *Revue des Jeunes.* Some sermons at the Church of the Madeleine treated 'the heroic life of the believer',[8] while others addressed public affairs. In 1918 he was elected a member of the Académie des Sciences Morales et Politiques.

The same year in a powerful sermon he expressed publicly the reticence of the French towards the peace plan of Pope Benedict XV sent to the heads of the Central and Allied Powers in August, 1917. (Great Britain showed interest in it, while the United States issued a refusal.) Sertillanges' critique of the papal initiative found considerable approbation among members of the French episcopacy and government; the sermon had received a prior approval from Cardinal Amette, Archbishop of Paris. 'However', reports historian André Duval, 'severe blame was expressed almost immediately by the Cardinal Secretary of State Pietro Gasparri who demanded sanctions from the Cardinal and the Rector of the Institut Catholique'.[9] After the death of Benedict XV in 1922, the Dominican became the target of a process in Rome. (Did suspicions of progressive thinking also play a role?)[10] Rome blocked Sertillanges from residing or publishing in France, producing an exile lasting seventeen years. 'The political tenor of one sermon in 1917 led to his suspension from the ministry after 1922 and to successive exiles . . . until 1939.'[11]

---

grace of Christ is becoming a social grace' (101). Sertillanges published in 1900 a critical edition of Claude Bernard's *Introduction à la médecine expérimentale* (Paris: Levé, 1900) with seventy-five pages of notes (Moos, 'Préface', 14).

7. *Saint Thomas d'Aquin* (Paris: Alcan, 1910) 2 volumes; *La philosophie morale de s. Thomas d'Aquin* (Paris: Alcan, 1916).

8. *La vie héroïque* (Paris: Bloud and Gay, 1914).

9. Duval, 'Sertillanges', 670. The sermon was published as *La paix française* (Paris: Bloud and Gay, 1918).

10. For documentation on the process see Antonio Piolanti, 'P. Antonin-Dalmace Sertillanges, O.P. Un tomista da non dimenticare', 79–90.

11. Vicaire, 'Sertillanges', 126; Duval, 'Sertillanges', 669.

After a year at the École Biblique in Jerusalem the exiled Dominican taught moral theology in Ryckholt, Holland (a school for Dominicans in exile) from 1924 to 1928 and then for ten years after 1929 at Le Saulchoir, the theological school of the Paris Province located at that time in Belgium. In 1939, the Master General of the Dominicans, Martin Gillet, convinced Pius XII to let him return to France where he took up his preaching and writing once again. After World War II he wrote new books; despite weak health, he devoted his strength to speaking engagements, dying on July 26, 1948.

M-D Chenu recalled:

> The Saulchoir when I arrived there had found its inspiration, methods, and balance through the gifts of many men who, living in the church of France in the midst of the modernist crisis, had serenely and solidly fashioned a theology holding for a scientific expression, contemplative fullness, and apostolic expression.[12]

The original inspiration of that school (which Chenu would make famous) came from Ambroise Gardeil (1859–1931) who in the words of Yves Congar 'was a thinker of the highest level in theology intent upon raising the quality of studies to a university level'.[13] Gardeil was Regent of Studies for many years and in 1901 offered a plan for a school of theology that would combine training in preaching and pastoral ministry with scientific methods in philosophy and theology as well as an openness to society and the university milieu. He developed important journals, and his book *Le Donné Révélé et la Théologie* set out the program for a dialogue between Aquinas and contemporary philosophy, while later books

---

12. Olivier de la Brosse, *Le Père Chenu: La liberté dans la foi* (Paris: Cerf, 1969), 24.

13. Jean-Pierre Jossua, *Le Père Congar: La théologie au service du peuple de Dieu* (Paris: Cerf, 1967), 17; see Henri-Dominique Gardeil, *L'Oeuvre théologique du P. Ambroise Gardeil* (Étiolles: Le Saulchoir, 1956); C de Belloy, 'Ambroise Gardeil: un combat pour l'étude', in *Frères Prêcheurs: Une Vocation Universitaire? Revue des sciences philosophiques et théologiques* 92 (2008), 423–432; Gerald McCool, in *The Neo-Thomists* (Milwaukee: Marquette University Press, 1994), 43–74. Avery Dulles whose survey omits Sertillanges wrongly sees Reginald Garrigou-Lagrange as the successor to Gardeil in apologetics (*A History of Apologetics* [New York: Corpus, 1971], 212). Another disciple of Gardeil was Marie-Dominique Roland-Gosselin; his writings from 1910 to 1913 pursued a less transcendental Thomism, a vital application of Aristotle and a look at ways in which Aquinas' philosophy of activity extends knowing.

brought together psychology and mysticism. Chenu referred to Gardeil's books as the source par excellence for the theological method and intellectual work at Le Saulchoir.

Along with Gardeil the three figures of Pierre Mandonnet, Antoine Lemonnyer, and Sertillanges gave seminal influences for the intellectual direction of the members of the Province of France. In September 1945 Sertillanges preached at the Saulchoir a retreat of conferences that were meditations on his experience of Dominican life. Chenu observed that the older Dominican's

> accomplishments along with the difficulties of exile gave him
> a spontaneous communion with the generation of young
> teachers at that time. Later the uncommon generosity with
> which Sertillanges tolerated the testing and disgrace he had
> undergone was not only a lesson in human moral life but a
> witness to the harshness of reality.[14]

In his journals Congar mentioned Sertillanges as the victim of unjust persecution. The Master General of the Dominican Order, Emmanuel Suarez, spoke in 1948 to Congar of what he had gained from Sertillanges and of Pius XII's admiration for Sertillanges' writings.[15] When Suarez singled him out with Lagrange as someone who despite false accusations had remained faithful and tried to do their work, Congar pointed out that in fact Sertillanges unfortunately always remained under a cloud until his death in 1948. 'I sensed at times a repression of ideas and persons . . . one from which Sertillanges never escaped suspicion.'[16] Karl Rahner listed Sertillanges with Maurice Blondel, Pierre Rousselot, and Max Scheler as furthering the view that Catholic thought should be receptive to modern philosophy.[17]

---

14. De la Brosse, *Le Père Chenu*, 25. 'At the time the Institut Catholique de Paris celebrated the centenary of his birth, Père Chenu said that generosity was the key to the life and work of Sertillanges.' (*De la vie: Pensées inédites de A.-D. Sertillanges, O.P.* [Ezanville: Gouin, 1984], 37).

15. *Journal d'un théologien*, 1946-1956 (Paris: Cerf, 2000), 154.

16. *Ibid*, 185, 161. Étienne Fouilloux, editor of Congar's journals, wonders if Sertillanges' long exile may have been due not just to papal displeasure but to other issues (*Journal d'un théologien*, 196, 238, 359, 427).

17. P Imhof and H Egan, *Karl Rahner in Dialogue: Conversations and Interviews, 1965–1982* (New York: Crossroad, 1986), 14.

A Theological Project

The historian M-D Vicaire estimated Sertillanges' writings at over 700 entries.[18] Their themes range from medicine to family education, from Calvary to papacy, but most fall into three large groups: (1) apologetics, (2) the philosophy of Aquinas, and (3) spirituality.

1. Apologetics. A new way of engaging non-believers was emerging in France. Apologetics was moving away from a logical chain of arguments to prove the existence of God or the reality of Jesus' miracles. Life and culture were seen as preambles to faith. In contrast to an extrinsic and rational argumentation, a new apologetic approach appealing to emotions, to intellect, and to the totality of the person's life, became prominent. Maurice Blondel wrote how reflection on immanence and consciousness pointed to religion, to God, and to the supernatural.[19] In a sense Sertillanges' entire oeuvre is a theological apologetic: sermons, reflections on Renaissance paintings, the ethics of Aquinas, and conversations with science—all are paths to God, to revelation and to the church.

In 1904, his small book on art and morality stressed the independence and synchronicity of both. The art of Florence or of Chartres can become paths to the transcendent, for art is a kind of incarnation of a historical culture. A work of three hundred pages published in 1909, *Art et Apologétique,* looked at cultural periods of art: not only at Biblical subjects, but at forms to see how they relate to Christian themes and to the religious search of the individual. *La Cathédrale: Sa Mission Spirituelle, Son Esthétique, Son Décor, Sa Vie*[20] from 1922 showed similarities among Gothic art, scholastic theology, and medieval mysticism. A further apologetic for faith collects texts on belief and the spiritual life from writers past and present and then links them to masterpieces of art ranging from mosaics

---

18. Vicaire, 'Sertillanges, Antonin Gilbert', 125.
19. L Maisonneuve, 'Apologétique (Méthodes nouvelles au XIXe Siècle)', in *Dictionnaire de théologie catholique* 1:2 (Paris: Letouzey et Ané, 1931), 1576–78. Maurice Lelong noted the prominence of 'life' in the titles of Sertillanges' writings (*De la vie*, 13); he gives a spirituality of the invisible, of nature, and of contemporary events. The universe does not display a rigid unity but one of development; similarly human life embraces liberty, faith, reason, and love. "Let us meditate on events where we meet this mystery of God in time: the accidental fades, evil redresses itself, the imperfect improves, the incomplete achieves, not in the visible always but in the ineffable" (*De la vie*, 218).
20. (Paris: Laurens, 1922).

and medieval windows to Raphael and Poussin.[21] Sertillanges was critical of how shallow religious art had become in the nineteenth century (evident in the shops around Saint Sulpice with their too colorful and too realistic images in church decoration), and he argued for legitimate developments of art whether in past times or in modern approaches.[22] 'The true artist is not simply the interpreter of the psychological state surrounding an individual soul. He is a burning mirror which receives light and concentrates it into a flame, a voice crying what everyone thinks in an unclear obscure way.'[23] In the tension between art, religion, and modernity three things are at work influencing each other: life, the religious aspect of life, and the expression of religious life in art.[24] Sertillanges published a range of dialogical works ranging from a catechism for non-believers in 1930 to a consideration of *Christianisme et les Philosophies* in 1940.

Today some of the writings on apologetics and the Christian life appear to be spirituality: collections of meditations, spiritual aphorisms, and prayers like *Rectitude* and *Récollection*. *L'Univers et l'Âme* and *Le Métier d'Homme* present a practical Christian anthropology. A particularly successful book was *The Intellectual Life*. Its chapters treat the intellectual life as a religious call, the organisation of a work in progress, and the sense of mystery in the creative process. The researcher and writer should know how to relax and how to stay in contact with ordinary life. A Thomistic emphasis upon the value of the individual and upon the ordinariness of artistic inspiration and divine grace runs through its pages as it turns creativity into spirituality.[25]

2. The Thought of Thomas Aquinas. By 1900 his study of Aquinas had approached the high level associated with the French Dominican school. Respect for Aquinas sets aside every ideology and monopoly; he has a

---

21. *La Foi* (Paris: Renouard, 1913).
22. *L'Art et la morale* (Paris: Bloud, 1904); he argued for the legitimate role of nude figures in modern art.
23. *Art et apologétique* (Paris: Bloud, 1909), 317.
24. *Art et apologétique,* 321. The arts of music are 'sacramental', not just an aid to grace but a fullness of reality that is graced. Church music should not be limited to chant and polyphony but should include modern ensembles of instruments (*Prière et musique* [Paris: Spes, 1938], 10, 66).
25. For a presentation of this book see the 'Foreword' by Richard Scholl in a new printing of *The Intellectual Life: Its Spirit, Conditions, Methods* (Washington, DC: The Catholic University of America Press, 1998), vii–xvi.

singular position among philosophers and theologians precisely because his principles do not reject all other thinkers nor do his works claim to say everything. Sertillanges' exposition of Aquinas—it remains largely within philosophy—is engaging and respectful of both its subject and its audience. The two volumes of *S. Thomas d'Aquin* begin with philosophical themes of being, nature, and the human life of thought, will, and action, while the subsequent presentation of ethics follows the Second Part of the *Summa Theologiae*—but abstractly, without much reference to modern ethical issues. In the treatment of virtues there is no mention of grace, no distinction between infused and acquired virtues, and no allusions to the Holy Spirit and its gifts—an approach typical of texts in moral theology from the first decades of the twentieth century.[26] Sertillanges stressed the totality, the systematic and dynamic aspects of Thomistic thought, and the contributions of students of Aquinas from the past. Aquinas had his medieval themes and systems, and yet that theology is capable of new developments; his thought-forms and ideas are like a living being growing and expanding.[27] Sertillanges wanted to explain Aquinas to those pursuing modern thought and to show that there are many ways to be a Thomist. The student of Aquinas should know the modern world.

Sertillanges directed a new French translation of the *Summa Theologiae* with commentaries. He himself did the volumes on God, creation, and the destiny of the human person,[28] treating creation mainly from the point of view of philosophical issues. His commentary in the notes indicates a creative mind at work; for instance, there is the insight that the created variety of finite beings in act mirrors the infinity of the divine being. Appendices hold some information drawn from patristic and conciliar sources. His small book on Aquinas from 1931, translated into German and English,[29] marked an advance over neo-Thomist manuals

---

26. See Thomas O'Meara, 'Interpreting Thomas Aquinas: Aspects of the Dominican School of Moral Theology in the Twentieth Century', in Stephen Pope, editor, *The Ethics of Aquinas* (Washington, DC: Georgetown University Press, 2002), 355–74.

27. Saint Thomas d'Aquin, *Somme Théologique: la création*, 2: 327–325 (Tournai: Éditions de la Revue des Jeunes, 1927).

28. Saint Thomas d'Aquin, *Somme Théologique: la création*, 1a, questions 44–49 (Tournai: Éditions de la Revue des Jeunes, 1927); see *L'Idée de création et ses retentissements en philosophie* (Paris: Aubier, 1945). There are also smaller books on the theses of Thomism, and collections of prayers and engaging passages selected from Aquinas' writings.

29. *Saint Thomas d'Aquin* (Paris: Flammarion, 1931).

as it presented not only Aquinas' goal and method but his personality as a thinker and as a poet, and a theology of the human person living in grace. Sertillanges was increasingly critical of any Thomism apart from historical knowledge, any mere metaphysics. The last two chapters treat Aquinas in contemporary culture and in the future. 'The modern revival of Thomism must be both a renewal and an effort to go deeper into St. Thomas' meaning.'[30] Aquinas' thought too is illumined by art. 'There is a real musical symmetry about the *Summa*, not because of some artifice in the distribution of its materials, but in its very structure: it emerges like a Gothic cathedral, a lyric of pure thought.'[31] A final chapter on Aquinas' poetry, mainly the Office for *Corpus Christi*, remains an unusual survey of how some French literary figures saw these texts.

> In reading his poetry we are struck by its austerity, its terseness and the avoidance of all unnecessary variety. It reads like a piece of music without accentuated pauses or unexpected marks of crescendo. It reminds one of Bach's first prelude without the false *Ave Maria* or his eighth prelude resounding through a cathedral.[32]

Sertillanges dreamt of a *Summa* of the future, one holding the principles of Aquinas in dialogue with humanity. He had moved Thomism from a philosophical summary to a cultural theology. For many, in the decades after 1930, that vivid and cultured presentation made Aquinas come alive.

3. *A Creative Spirit.* His correspondence and a book of lectures illustrate his contemporary openness. Sertillanges received in 1934 a letter from Pierre Teilhard de Chardin (who also came from Clermont-Ferrand) writing from China.

> I just read your valuable little book *Dieu ou Rien* which has reached our distant shores. It gave me great joy. Your voice, so measured yet commanding, makes me hear again the approach that I have dreamt of, for a long time: to express something in a fresh way. I am certain of this: If Christianity often has so little influence in the consciousness of believers

---

30. *Saint Thomas Aquinas and His Work* (London: Burns and Oates, 1933), 131.
31. *Saint Thomas Aquinas,* 113.
32. *Saint Thomas Aquinas,* 117.

and fails to attract the soul of non-believers, this is mainly
because it carries an air of disdaining or fearing the grandeur
and unity of our universe . . . Christ is re-incarnating himself, for our mind and our heart, in the formidable dimensions of what is recently discovered of the experienced Real.
These dimensions, almost without measure—Christ must
be capable of reaching and illuminating them. I think that
St. Thomas would appreciate the joyous daring with which
you see things expanding a little more, each day, before us.
It is good to feel around oneself, in the church, like-thinking
companions at arms.[33]

The following year saw the Dominican collecting and studying the unpub-
lished, privately circulated texts of Teilhard.[34] Sertillanges agreed with the
enterprise of 'our dear Père Teilhard' and its 'magnificent expansiveness',[35]
although he warned against identifying the Incarnation too solidly with
the result or climax of evolution. Is it sufficiently clear how Christian charity proceeds out of the long biological history of the evolution of a species? 'Père Teilhard de Chardin does not come up short but perhaps he
has exceeded [the limits of faith and science]. I think so. Nevertheless,
he has said some admirable things and what he concludes in terms of an
apologetic perspective is worth serious consideration.'[36] In general, evolution aims at the human being and at the honor and responsibility of our
species. The idea of evolution is not foreign to Aquinas for whom the individual progresses and unfolds, but not the species. 'It would be possible
that the act [of the Creator], establishing itself in a lengthy and observable
duration, is less occupied with making beings and things through a direct
activity as letting other beings themselves fashion them.'[37]

A remarkable effort of this Dominican is a series of lectures published
in 1913 as a book on feminism: *Féminisme et Christianisme*. The word has
a history in Europe in the nineteenth century, and in France the rights
of women debated and enacted in the century after Napoleon are what

---

33. Moos, 'Préface', 16f.

34. See *Dieu ou rien* (Paris: Flammarion, 1933), I, 52–68.

35. 'L'Évolution dans la doctrine de saint Thomas et la pensée du Père Teilhard de Chardin', *L'Univers et l'âme*, 23.

36. 'L'Évolution dans la doctrine de saint Thomas', 21, 46

37. *L'Idée de création et ses retentissements en philosophie*, 140.

some experts call 'the first feminism'.[38] The book comprises ten addresses (curiously, each begins, 'Gentlemen') whose themes range from the origins of the feminist movement and the place of the Christian message in feminine liberation to feminist principles and Christian principles, work, politics, marriage, divorce, and education. After showing how feminism comes out of political and social movements of the nineteenth century, Sertillanges stressed that a feminist movement is understandable as a force in human life during the early twentieth century. Societies change as they understand justice differently. Every aspect of true liberation must be encouraged, and all classes of society should change. Women should enter the professions they can perform.[39] Feminism should not develop without men being part of the movement. He mentioned that Engels spoke of the great historical defeat of the female sex. 'That defeat in the past is not deniable, but in Christian terms that past failure is like original sin. The arrival of Jesus has challenged and removed sin in a basic way; the effects of sin will continue to be challenged to the extent the Gospel reigns.'[40]

Christianity at its origins was an immense revolutionary movement, and this revolution can be found at each stage in history. To respect the memory of the past is not to repress the power of the Christian reality. The religious principle is not a drug but a viaticum for the road, directing, promoting a march forward, and eschewing prudence and stagnation. Sertillanges did not escape the limitations of his age as he mentioned the pattern of complementarity and an inevitable inequality in business, national politics, and church. He concluded: 'Let us rejoice as Christians in this aspiration. Christianity has here, as always, a necessary role . . . The Gospel is for all times; one must not nail it down. It is not a lantern attached to a pole but a fire.'[41]

A Theology of the Church in the Century of the Church

A large work, *The Church,* was published in 1917. Its style and content lie far beyond a work like the *Tractatus de Ecclesia Christi ad Mentem S. Thomae Aquinatis* from 1949 by another French Dominican, Gérard Par-

---

38. See Colleen Guy, 'France', in Helen Tierney, *Women's Studies Encyclopedia* (Westport: Greenwood Press, 1999), 1, 532.
39. *Féminisme et christianisme* (Paris: Gabalda, 1913; republished in 1930), 20.
40. *Féminisme et christianisme,* 67.
41. *Féminisme et christianisme,* 30.

is.[42] That neo-Thomist ecclesiology did not draw much from Aquinas' theology but offered an Aristotelian theory of ecclesiastical causalities. The formal cause of the church is the bishops; the remote efficient cause is Jesus or the Holy Spirit; the proximate efficient cause is the bishops; the final cause is heaven. The mainly passive material cause is any baptised person who does not hold a church office. Sertillanges went beyond such ecclesiastical mechanics.[43] His modern ecclesiology, which could be seen as a philosophical theology of religion, also unfolds the relationships of the Roman Catholic Church to culture and to other churches and religions. 'The church must not be studied with the superficial glance of a passer-by, still less with the prejudiced gaze that sees nothing but faults and fearful forces claiming power everywhere; rather the perspective should be as wide as the horizon of humanity.'[44]

This theology of the church from within, a somewhat modern perspective, treats in its opening pages topics like religious feeling, the supernatural reality within Christianity, and the social dimension of Christianity. Book Two looks at the traditional four marks of the church and then at the government and authority of the church. Book Three considers the seven sacraments and some sacramentals including almsgiving, the word of God, indulgences, and (curiously) the Mass. Book Four studies the relationships of the church to the world, to religions and churches, and to art and politics. The final book returns to the organisation of the church, to the pope, the magisterium, and to priestly, episcopal, and monastic 'orders'. Thus his ecclesiology seeks to meet in a general way the modern issues bearing upon the structure of the Roman Catholic Church.

The human race has an organic mode of being and a developmental dynamic. Humanity will never reach a point where religion will be unnecessary (as some think); inner feelings of piety and art, religious if not Christian, can point to a high notion of God. A supernatural faith has a future and a message for the future. 'A true Christian should not be one of those who favor hanging back and also not someone who rushes forward so quickly that they leave the battle behind them . . . Catholicism has an

---

42. (Malta: Muscat, 1949). This approach reappears in Charles Journet's analysis of church authorities as efficient causes; see O'Meara, 'The Teaching Office of Bishops in the Ecclesiology of Charles Journet', in *The Jurist* 49 (1989): 23–47.
43. *The Church* (New York: Benziger Brothers, 1922), ix [*L'Église* (Paris: Lecoffre, 1917), 2 volumes].
44. *The Church*, 392.

indefinite life stretching before it. This life must be a progress, a progress in dogma, in religious discipline, in morals, in everything.'[45] The church is the result of the social development of human beings, and its human and divine aspects compose an organism animated by the Holy Spirit. The venerable but static four marks of the church yield to aspects of this organic dynamic. This ecclesiology of organism and Spirit is not unrelated to that of Johann Adam Möhler whom the Dominican had studied.[46]

Nevertheless, Sertillanges' ecclesiology holds only a modest idea of seminal development. The church of the first century in its organisational structure is essentially the same as that of modern times. His vision of the church is limited by the lack of examples of anything new and by little treatment of variations in past history. Claiming to be apostolic and progressive, his ecclesiology remains abstract; although the church's nature is to discover the truth, it stays apart from change.

> Thanks to the Spirit, the universal church, as varied as it is in its local forms and tendencies, is always the church. It develops permanence in ways similar to ways living species do. Its essential directing idea is unchangeable and is present in the lines where the church advances, like a band of soldiers in one forward movement. Its dogma, its morality, its discipline, its sacramental liturgy, its hierarchical constitution are essentially in the twentieth century what they were under St. Paul, what they were at the Upper Room.[47]

Several chapters examine church authority. What reason and law are to public society, the Holy Spirit is to the church, its vital principle. 'The action of the Spirit is not exclusively to be found in our chiefs, although in

---

45. *The Church*, 102.
46. Sertillanges wrote an essay, 'Religion et Universalité', for the volume edited by the Jesuit Pierre Chaillet which was to reintroduce the French church to the Tübingen theologian (*L'Église est Une: Homage à Moehler* [Paris: Bloud and Gay, 1939]). The essay is a reflection on the nature of religions in history, and its concluding section echoes Möhler in the explanation of 'catholic' as finding the church in a 'humanity organized in God by Christ' with and beyond individuality in a global universality and a long temporality (32); see Thomas O'Meara, 'Beyond "Hierarchology": Johann Adam Möhler and Yves Congar', in Donald J Dietrich and Michael J Himes editors, *The Legacy of the Tübingen School: The Relevance of Nineteenth-Century Theology for the Twenty-First Century* (New York: Crossroad, 1997), 173–91.
47. (Paris: Flammarion, 1930), 83.

this case they are promised a special assistance . . . [It] is diffused through the whole church, giving life to the faithful and breathing truth into them, affording them grace and useful impulses, listening as well as speaking.'[48] The church is not a solitary monarchy influenced by no one. 'Is it an autocracy in the full and exclusive sense of the word? Such a being would be a monster or else a maniac. Every regime of persons is modified by various collaborations without which it would become the most unsupportable tyranny.'[49] Excessive authority has no right to be obeyed. The people are basically the church, and authority exists to serve ecclesial association and to promote collaboration. 'The church prescribes a path for us, but she cannot walk it on our behalf, nor even lead us in that way.'[50] The church offers the sacraments but does not create or own them. The church will not succeed if it has lost the good will of the people, if it depends on authoritarianism, if it loses sight of the activity of God in men and women. The church should have some aspects of a 'democracy'—Sertillanges used the word—like elections and associations; cooperation and participation will fashion a better community life. People make up the church.

This theology of the church from the time of World War I looks directly not only at other Christian churches but also at the world religions. 'Outside the church no salvation' is a truth—but only a partial truth needing complementary truths. Those in other religions, past and present, belong to the 'soul of the church'[51] and live in a grace of God that is broad. There is a 'wide Catholicity'[52] inviting all to salvation. Religions help people who have goodness and grace in them belong to the soul of the church. His theology was not surprisingly, considering the times, occasionally vague. 'These non-Catholic religions do not give grace; but they may occasion it, guard it, or aid it to grow.'[53] Interestingly, Sertillanges was more creative and sympathetic in his reflections on world religions than in his thoughts about Orthodox and Protestant churches. An apologetic mentality saw

---

48. *The Church*, 334. Still, a move away from church authority is a move away from the church and the Gospel to where the critical and disobedient person ends up alone (133).
49. *The Church*, 332.
50. *The Church*, 336.
51. *The Church*, 250. 'We must say and maintain, in the name of dogmatic truth, *Outside the church no salvation*. But we must clearly understand that if by the word *church* we mean the visible group that enrolled Catholics make up, the formula . . . is no more than an official truth which life outruns in every direction, and in which the Spirit . . . will not agree to be found' (*The Church*, 260).
52. *The Church*.
53. *The Church*, 255.

easily the defects of other churches in Europe, while, on the other hand, a theology of grace as the soul of the church steps in to provide wide salvation for those outside the institutional church.

In 1933, Sertillanges published a smaller book on the church in history. History here means the first centuries of the church's life: the stages of the church before the church, the birth of the church, the church's development followed by the church in today's world.[54] He stressed the original Jewish ideas as well as the Hellenic and Roman religious movements and realities that enabled the church to expand.

> What is lacking to the Israelite embryo is the Christian soul; this will be infused when the Spirit descends, socializing the personal gifts made to Jesus of his divinity, and realizing in this the point of departure of authentic life in religion.[55]

The covenant with Israel has a special role, and yet other religions also make their positive contributions to Christianity. This book too retains the motif of the seed: a seed of progress not repressed by modernity, a seed possessing an original fullness and an abundant expansion. The Pauline letters through the various words for leadership (bishop, priest, apostle) show development in the New Testament church, 'a fluidity in the reality'[56] of church offices before they are stabilised in the next generation around 100 AD. The plant (church offices, liturgies) grows from the seed in the decades after Pentecost, although 'accessories to which we are accustomed . . . a little version of the college of cardinals, a little office of the Index'[57] would not be present.

The book stays focused on the early church; only a dozen pages reflect on the 'Church at the Present Time' in terms of change and stabil-

---

54. *Le Miracle de l'église* (Paris: Spes, 1933); a number of works like *Socialisme et christianisme* (Paris, Lecoffre, 1905) treat contemporary social movements. 'The church should have a tendency to embrace the world for the purpose of enriching the world with its gifts. Respectful of all those powers [in society], it will seek to reclaim for itself only the liberty of service. Because that service is in its eyes the most dominant and the most sacred of its duties, it will defend at any price, and against all, the principles grounding its freedom for service' ('Et Toi, Que Penses-Tu de l'Église?', in *La Revue des Jeunes* 17 [1927]: 18).
55. *Le Miracle de l'église*, 35.
56. *Le Miracle de l'église*, 110, 46.
57. *Le Miracle de l'église*, 88, 90.

ity. Sertillanges finds himself arguing against the entry into the life of the church of what is 'extrinsic' or 'novel' (secular or Protestant forms and ideas). The papacy, despite its lack of a territory, army, and powerful civil organisation, has survived and will survive. It will survive even Mussolini and Hitler now threatening the Vatican.[58] The church is the instrument of providence, of the reign of God; it knows how to bring good out of evil, how to continue to be a source of what is holy. The church should support what is truly human.

> The more there is of humanity in the church the more there must be of divinity precisely so that the human can exist; and, as more of divinity enters the human being, free and responsible efforts will recognize limits and imperfections . . . even as it serves the holiness of the church which is latent divinity.[59]

Conclusion

A systematisation of Aquinas' thinking, an apologetics using art, sermons on social and political issues, a theology of the church amid a history of religions, an open dialogue with Bergson and Teilhard de Chardin—these indicate an unusual thinker from the first half of the twentieth century. The contemporary world attracted rather than frightened him. He never fled the prophetic responsibility of looking at Christian revelation in ways that were both old and new. He delivered his lectures and wrote his books and articles in an era when the mechanics of church law, neo-scholastic logic, and an all-directing papal governance are present in a formidable and even frightening way. Although it is difficult to sum up the many publications, a conclusion of Reginaldo Omez has merit: 'The fundamental idea in Sertillanges is that all knowledge and every activity are permeated with religion.'[60] Religion is not a mental faith nor a past revelation, but a reality in culture. Themes of seminal realities, organic life, the divine in the human, and culture explain the church today. When reading his writings one does not imagine a solitary believer in a dimly lit cathedral, but a teacher in local community in dialogue with its society and active through many ministries.

---

58. *Le Miracle de l'église*, 232.
59. *Le Miracle de l'église*, 237–39.
60. Omez, 'Sertillanges, Antonin-Gilbert', in *Enciclopedia Cattolica* 11 (1953): 403.

Chapter 2

M-D Chenu: Situating Theology in History

Marie-Dominique Chenu was an extraordinary figure in many ways. His long life (1895–1990) allowed him to sow ideas across several generations. He not only mastered his chosen field of history but also influenced the cognate areas of dogmatic and pastoral theology. With a warm personality and generous heart he reached out to a range of colleagues and friends from the erudite to the unsophisticated. One author claims, 'It would be very difficult to write an accurate history of twentieth-century Catholicism without granting a pivotal role to the contributions of French theologian Marie-Dominique Chenu'.[1] He was the friend and colleague of great theologians and he influenced and challenged many of them. During the Second Vatican Council he played a creative role as well. Chenu was sure of himself and confident enough to take risks for the future.

Probably Chenu's most important contribution was in the development of Le Saulchoir where he mentored theologians, exegetes, and church historians who helped lay the foundations for Vatican II. The Bishop of Madagascar, a former student, invited Chenu to Vatican II as his personal theological expert. Once there, Chenu's renown as a historian and theologian brought him into the circle of key players at the council (among them, Congar, Lebret, and Liégé, studied elsewhere in this book).

Although professionally devoted to research in medieval philosophy and theology, Chenu was also involved in the social and pastoral renewal of the church. As a historian and a theologian, Chenu felt a responsibility to be in creative dialogue with contemporary social currents. Evidence of this conviction can be found in this self-description from 1969: 'In a

---

1. Christophe F Potworowski, *Contemplation and Incarnation: The Theology of Marie-Dominique Chenu* (Montreal and Kingston: McGill-Queen's University Press, 2001), xi.

field that might be called *sociological history*, I am a historian of the gospel among the people of God and concerned about the exact intersection where the gospel becomes yeast for the life of the Church. That is where divine mystery and the Holy Spirit are at work.'[2] This is not conventional theological language. But it reveals Chenu's strengths as well as what some considered his weakness. Always claiming to base himself upon concrete experiences of normal people, he nonetheless reserved the right to flights of prophetic exhortation. His most remarkable student and colleague, Yves Congar, once remarked, 'Père Chenu is a perpetual eruption of ideas!' With solid theological understanding and historical insight, Chenu tried to reframe the social and pastoral questions of his day. In some cases, his efforts resulted in initiatives that have remained classic resources for contemporary theology.

Background and Formation

Chenu was born on 7 January 1895, in Soisy-sur-Seine, a town south of Paris that hugs the banks of the Seine River. His father owned a factory for bandsaws. Chenu was baptised Marcel-Léon and grew up in this unremarkable neighborhood that four decades later would become the site of Le Saulchoir, the theological school whose most famous master he would become. Religiously inclined as a boy, Chenu entered the diocesan seminary of Versailles at the age of seventeen, but decided to become a Dominican friar in the following year.[3]

At that time the Dominican house of studies was located in Belgium, because the Order of Preachers, like other religious, had been expelled from France in 1904. The place was called Le Saulchoir after a stand of willows (*saules* in French) in the yard. The building, not far from Tournai, had been a monastery for Cistercian nuns. When the Dominicans returned to France in 1937, they transplanted the name to Étiolles (just two kilometers from where Chenu grew up), and that name has since been transferred to the present Dominican library for theological research in the thirteenth arondissement of Paris where books and papers that Chenu, Congar, and their colleagues had worked with are housed and consulted by scholars today.

---

2. *La Vie spirituelle*, 90 (September 1969): 288.
3. See *Jacques Duquesne interroge le Père Chenu: Un théologien en liberté* (Paris: Centurion, 1975), especially chapter 2. References hereafter will be indicated simply as *Duquesne*.

Becoming a Dominican

In the novitiate in 1913 Chenu adopted the religious name Dominique, adding the prefix Marie, as was the custom then. Thereafter he signed himself Marie-Dominique or M-D Chenu. He made his first profession in 1914, at the age of 19. Then, because the war had broken out and his health was too poor for military service, Chenu was sent to Rome where he studied philosophy, theology, history, and biblical studies at the University of Saint Thomas Aquinas, known as the Angelicum.[4] In 1920 he concluded his studies by writing a doctoral thesis under the prominent Dominican theologian Réginald Garrigou-Lagrange. His thesis treated the psychological and theological aspects of contemplation and it anticipates theological tendencies that would shape Chenu's entire career.[5]

Garrigou-Lagrange was impressed with his protégé and invited Chenu to remain at the Angelicum as his assistant. However, Chenu had acquired a taste for a different kind of theology, and he returned to Le Saulchoir. There Chenu fell under the influence of two great minds that would permanently influence his intellectual work, Ambroise Gardeil who stressed the supremacy of the revealed sources of theology and Pierre Mandonnet who introduced Chenu to the historical study of medieval texts.[6] In Rome, Garrigou-Lagrange was not happy about this, not only because he was losing a student whom he had counted on as an assistant, but also because he was losing Chenu to a historically oriented project that he considered wrong-headed.

As events would demonstrate, Garrigou-Lagrange became the symbol of an outdated non-historical, essentialistic theology that refused to adapt to changing times and cultural challenges. By contrast, Chenu became the avatar of a revival of theological creativity nourished by historical sources and pastoral sensitivity. Having already spent one year at the Saulchoir as a novice, Chenu was enticed back by its allure. Years later, he quipped humorously, 'If I had stayed in Rome, perhaps I'd be a cardinal now!'[7] He

---

4. *Jacques Duquesne interroge le Père Chenu,* 29f.
5. CG Conticello, editor, '*De Contemplatione* (Angelicum, 1920): La thèse inédite de doctorat du Père M.-D. Chenu', in *Revue des sciences philosophiques et théologiques* 75 (1991): 363–422. See the analysis of Chenu's thesis by Potworowski, *Contemplation and Incarnation,* 6f.
6. Olivier de la Brosse, *Le Père Chenu: La liberté dans la foi* (Paris: Éditions du Cerf, 1969), 23f.
7. *Jacques Duquesne interroge le Père Chenu,* 39.

didn't stay, though, and he never came close to being a cardinal.

Becoming a History-Oriented Theologian

By the 1920s, Le Saulchoir had acquired its characteristic style. The key-stone of its program was found in Gardeil's most famous work *Le Donné Révélé et la Théologie (Revealed Data and Theology)*. Gardeil held that in order to renew theology, you have to go back to its sources, above all the revealed source of sacred scripture. Chenu referred to Gardeil's book as the breviary of the Saulchoir's methodology, meaning that the Dominicans found there the spirit and perspective to guide their own study and writings.[8] While the seminaries used second hand and third hand accounts of the data of Scripture, the Fathers, and the councils of the church in manuals, the Dominican faculty used primary source texts. Pierre Mandonnet, noted for studies that placed the writings of St Thomas Aquinas in their historical and cultural perspective, provided the faculty with the methodology for this new orientation. A critical inquiry into the genesis of ideas was employed in every branch of ecclesiastical studies.

By 1932, Chenu assumed the post of Regent of Studies (the director of the students' study programs and head of the school). In 1937, the Dominican studium became a Pontifical University with two faculties of philosophy and theology, and Chenu himself became its first rector. The provincial, Père Padé, had arranged for its return to French soil. The new Le Saulchoir at Étiolles was roughly 20 miles south of Paris, allowing for an exchange of ideas between the Dominicans and mainstream university life. It was also close to the many research centers and specialised libraries in Paris.

Le Saulchoir educated quite a number of important theological personalities: not only Yves Congar, but also biblical scholars like Roland de Vaux and Pierre Benoît, liturgists like Pierre-Marie Gy and Irenée Dalmais, pastoral and moral theologians liked Albert Plé, Pierre Liégé and Pie Régamey, as well as scholars from other Dominican provinces like Edward Schillebeeckx, Gustavo Gutierrez (who was not a Dominican at the time), and Timothy Radcliffe.

Chenu taught a variety of courses at Le Saulchoir and was essentially the architect of its study program. He taught Congar Greek and later

---

8. M-D Chenu, *Une école de théologie: Le Saulchoir* (Kain-lez-Tournai and Étiolles: Le Saulchoir, 1937), 40. See also M Quisinsky, 'Echos allemands à Une école de théologie: Le Saulchoir de M.-D. Chenu', in *Revue des sciences philosophiques et théologiques* 94:1 (Jan-Mar, 2010): 121-132.

the history of dogma. Congar loved to reminisce about 'the marvelous impression of being awakened by Chenu, of coming to understand what people thought in the past, and there recognizing the vital stages in the development of theology'.[9] What people remember about Chenu above all is his warm encouragement, his sympathetic listening, his eager involvement in the creative thinking of others, and his partnership in finding resources for new areas of research. Following Chenu's example, it became the custom for the friars to pass to one another texts and articles that emerged from their research.

Not long after becoming Regent, Chenu undertook to articulate Le Saulchoir's program. This effort became his publication of 1937 entitled simply *Le Saulchoir: A School of Theology*.[10] In this small book of 128 pages, destined for circulation among friends and never placed in bookstores, he provided a history of the Dominican studium, pointing out the school's fidelity to the genius of Lacordaire and Gardeil. He spoke of the spirit and the method of its philosophical and theological teaching. Finally, he gave an appendix listing the publications of the members of the school—already a formidable list by 1937. This little work gave the impression not only of advocating a return to the sources, the methodology used at the school; but of arguing convincingly that such an approach was a serious methodology for twentieth century theology. It was an appeal to go back to the sources of Christian theology in order to do justice to the great medieval tradition of St. Thomas Aquinas and his commentators, and to allow their theology to enter into dialogue with contemporary culture.

The ecclesiastical context in 1937 was far from open to change. Roman authorities were suspicious of any novel formulations of thought and were still afraid of critical biblical scholarship and the remnants of French Modernism. In general, they mistrusted the use of history in theology and considered it a risk destined to lead to relativism by abandoning a timeless *philosophia perennis*. Chenu's booklet was delated to Rome along with denunciations made by ecclesiastics who disliked his approach, and there were personalities in Rome who were eager to see Chenu discredited. In 1942, the Vatican's Holy Office took Chenu's book out of circulation and expelled him from his post as director and professor at the Saulchoir.

There is an amusing, if grotesque, dimension to this story. Chenu had

---

9.   Jean-Pierre Jossua, *Le Père Congar: La théologie au service du peuple de Dieu* (Paris: Éditions du Cerf, 1967), 19.
10. See note 5 above.

warned in his booklet that St Thomas's theology should not be allowed to be turned into an 'orthodoxy', meaning (for Chenu) an official program from which no one would be permitted to deviate. So he was called to Rome and interrogated by personnel of the Holy Office about having claimed that St Thomas was not orthodox. Subtlety of thought was not the strong suit of the church's doctrinal watchdog.[11]

Congar once remarked that he could never understand how Chenu's work was so misrepresented and misunderstood in Rome. Clearly people in Rome thought that Chenu's description of Le Saulchoir's methodology might represent a return to the errors of Modernism condemned in the 1900s and 1910s, but there were also some who were looking for an opportunity to block his creative initiatives. Chenu had formed and directed a school that breathed intellectual freedom and that took pastoral problems seriously, emphasising participation, communication and practical engagement with the church. At that time, none of that was desirable in Rome. In any case, in 1942 Chenu's book was officially placed on the *Index of Forbidden Books* and removed from circulation. Chenu himself was sent to live at the Priory of Saint-Jacques in Paris and warned not to publish or to teach.

This left the Saulchoir without a head. Thomas Philippe became the Regent in Chenu's place—a man with a religious and pious rather than a properly theological charism. There were also internal conflicts; some members of the faculty felt that they needed to change the school's theological program as a result of Rome's displeasure. The Saulchoir lived under a cloud of suspicion, and it had lost the extraordinarily creative leadership that only Chenu could give to it. Provocative ideas in Chenu's book are easy enough to find. Here are two examples:

> The result of St. Thomas Aquinas's spiritual freedom, guiding his theological practice, was his attitude of *inventiveness* that allowed him to focus on the effervescent environment and the revolutionary intellectual spirit of the 13th century. To adopt this heritage and put it into practice was something of a risk around 1900, perhaps even imprudent. The lessons for our elders who were the Thomists of the 16th century had

---

11. De la Brosse, *Le Père Chenu*, 99. Cf *Duquesne*, 120: 'They made me sign a paper saying that St. Thomas really was orthodox. You can see the kind of persons involved! They had no feeling for real problems—they read everything through distorting lenses.'

been difficult: faced with the humanism of Erasmus, the religious revolution of Luther, the scientific revolution of Galileo, and later the philosophical revolution of Descartes, they barricaded themselves within their traditional verities so as to resist the assaults of a new age . . . [12]

However, a theology can't be built upon negations, but only according to its own appropriate principles and according to the internal hierarchy of its objects. This is an essential law for theological method. Doubtless this is the reason for the freedom with which Père Gardeil undertook what he himself called rather boldly 'the work of cleaning up the domain of theology'.[13]

Theology That Appeared Too Modern

Chenu's main points were clear. Theologians need to be in vital contact with contemporary developments in society. For an attentive theologian, the world and its cultural evolution must become a hermeneutic (a meaning-giving perspective) for understanding the word of God. Dominican professors at the Angelicum (particularly Garrigou-Lagrange) and Vatican officials in Rome found such expressions untenable. They seemed untraditional and unorthodox and capable of dangerous interpretations. However, they represented Chenu's frame of mind as an educator who wanted theology to be in touch with the real world. Chenu's troubles over his presentation of the program of his school of theology illustrate an essential fact about his life. By his situation in time and place he was a transitional figure. None of his work can be evaluated in a historical vacuum.

Earlier in Belgium, Chenu and other faculty members of Le Saulchoir had begun welcoming for dialogue, study and retreats the chaplains of the Young Christian Workers movement founded by Abbé Cardijn. Cardijn's initiative aimed to bring a fraternal missionary presence into the context of young adult working class people who felt alienated from the largely bourgeois atmosphere of the typical Catholic parish of the time. These pastors on the frontiers of the church's pastoral life paid Chenu the tribute of telling him: 'You help us to understand what we are really doing.'[14] Chenu was able to articulate the ecclesiology that was implicit in their

---

12. *Une école de théologie*, 44.
13. *Une école de théologie*, 52.
14. Jean-Pierre Jossua, *Le Père Congar*, 26.

approach to ministry. For example, in a conference addressed to chaplains of the Young Christian Workers, Chenu had said:

> The priesthood can't be defined only by its function of sacra-
> mentally continuing the mystery of Christ in established faith
> communities. It also has the missionary function of evange-
> lizing the nations. The priesthood is not only the framework
> of an already established church, it is also the organic en-
> ergy of the gospel among the nations. It is 'missionary', as the
> Instruction of the Congregation for the Propagation of the
> Faith makes clear.[15]

Chenu was insisting here on the *prophetic* mission of the ordained minister, something that will become one of the vibrant themes in the renewal
theology of Vatican II. Evangelisation, rediscovered at Vatican II, is already a vibrant part of Chenu's pastoral theology.

Chenu and his colleagues never lost sight of the context of the world.
Theology was an ongoing dialogue with real people who were struggling
to believe; it was a means to evangelise a world filled with challenges and
contradictions, not a dialogue with dead authors from a totally different
environment. Their daring self-confidence frightened the Roman Curia,
and that would remain the source of endless conflicts until the day that
Pope John's council introduced a new openness to the world of modernity
and human progress into the church. If Pope John XXIII made *aggiornamento* a motto for the council, surely one of the ideas he had in mind was
this transformation of theology from a diatribe against the modern world
into a dialogue with it.

Widening the Circle of Influence

In Belgium, under Mandonnet's influence, the school had founded a number of scholarly journals linked to the inauguration of a new Institute of
Medieval Studies within the Dominican studium in 1921. Chenu became
the mainstay of these publications, mastering the technical literature in
the field and editing articles by colleagues. The high quality of Chenu's
work soon became recognised by scholars in the field, especially by the

---

15. M-D Chenu, 'Le Sacerdoce des Prêtres Ouvriers', in *L'Évangile dans le Temps, Cogitatio Fidei* 11 (Paris: Éditions du Cerf, 1964), 279.

great medievalist, Professor Étienne Gilson of the Sorbonne, who became both Chenu's friend and partner.

In 1928, Gilson founded the Institute of Medieval Studies in Toronto and convinced Chenu to create a similar program in Ottawa. Accordingly, in 1930, the *Institut d'Études Médiévales* was founded in Ottawa. (After 1942, it became attached to the University of Montreal). Chenu became an influential figure in Canadian intellectual life as a result of annual visits to the institute in Ottawa. By attracting major North American talent to medieval studies and historical theology in the style of Le Saulchoir, the Canadian institute produced a large number of important monographs and articles, as well as a critical edition of the *Summa Theologiae* of St. Thomas in 1941. A number of North American Dominicans were influenced by Chenu and by his first students as a result of the Canadian institute.

An Extraordinary Outreach

André Duval, the Dominican historian and a student and friend of Chenu, once remarked that sending Chenu into exile was a relative term, because each time that he was forced to move, Chenu extended his circle of friends, groups, and networks. Chenu was exiled from Le Saulchoir; but as soon as Chenu arrived in Paris, his friend Gabriel Le Bras, the noted historian and sociologist, invited him to teach at *l'Ecole des Hautes Études* of the University of Paris, and he also helped Chenu to gain a position as professor at the *Institut Catholique* in Paris, a position that Chenu would hold for many years. He continued the research that he began before the war. In these university positions he would have the time and encouragement to organise and publish the scholarly material on which he had worked for decades, leading to his books *Introduction to the Study of Saint Thomas* (1950) and *Theology in the Twelfth Century* (1957), two works considered timeless masterpieces.

Paris opened up a new and different period of Chenu's life. Rome's aggressive attack on him in 1942 had come at the time of France's agonizing experience of the Second World War. The hardship and confusion of those days were bitter and difficult for everyone. It was a period of hard times for the church as well. Chenu, who had known and worked with the Young Christian Workers movement, began alliances with new pastoral and social initiatives in Paris and across France, for example, the *Semaines Sociales* (national study weeks on social questions), the programs of Père Lebret and *Économie et Humanisme,* the national *Centre de Pastorale*

Liturgique, as well as small groups, including bi-weekly or monthly meetings with Catholic leaders.

A Dominican colleague from that time tells a characteristic story about Chenu. 'One day', recounted Père Jomier, 'Chenu was hopelessly overcommitted and had to give up one of two meetings of Catholic Action groups that he had somehow scheduled for the same time. He decided to stay with the small group of families in his neighborhood and to pass up the other group composed of important lawyers and judges. "They have resources", he told me, "they can find another chaplain without any trouble. But if I abandon my neighborhood families here, nobody else will take care of them". Père Chenu's response has always been a source of amazement for me.'[16]

Years later after Vatican II, when the huge Saint-Jacques community had set up support groups of ten or twelve friars within the priory for monthly small group prayer, conversation and recreation, Chenu told his support group that he had been invited to the Elysée Palace (the president's residence) for a banquet. But he told the palace that he needed to refuse the president's invitation because it was the night for his *groupe de vie* at the priory. Chenu could identify his priorities.

However, an important episode of this period of Chenu's life in Paris, still full of academic and pastoral commitments, is Chenu's relationship to the priest worker movement. After World War II, there was a great pastoral effort to reach out to working-class people and to the unchurched called the *Mission de France*.[17] By the end of the 1940s, this effort developed in the direction of priest workers, namely, priests who took factory or blue collar jobs and lived and ministered in the neighborhoods of the poor. In his articles and conferences Chenu sketched out the essential dimensions of the question. As he put it, the working class was not so much *dechristianised* as *unevangelised*. The church had never made a serious effort to enter and inhabit the brutalising world of industrial labor. Tacitly it invited the working class into parishes that were essentially a foreign land from their point of view—bourgeois, comfortable and conservative. For all practical purposes, the church in France had abandoned the working poor and was unacquainted with and absent from their neighborhoods.

With the birth of Catholic Action and its hopes to develop an apostolic

---

16. De la Brosse, *Le Père Chenu*, 109, note 2.
17. Cf our chapter about Louis-Joseph Lebret. Cf *Duquesne*, chapter 7, 132f.

laity, however, the church started to become aware of its need to be present to the whole of society, even to the poor with all their diversity and their needs. Few pastors or bishops understood the cultural rift between the bourgeois life of the average parish and the material and social needs of workers and the truly poor. Chenu attempted to address this disconnect when he wrote:

> It is through the laity first of all that the church should be a witness among the working classes by means of the presence and activities of those who have no choice but to live and work there and to build community as members of the body of Christ. But the laity don't constitute the church all by themselves; the church in its fullness is both priesthood and laity. For the church to be present to this world of the working poor, the priest also has to be inserted there along with the laity. Priests have to be attentive to the people's problems, their questions, their needs, and observe and listen to make sure that the people hear the response that the church has to offer them. At a time like this when the laity are coming into their own, what is needed is a new type of priest who can provide this kind of availability, this presence to the world, this rapport in sharing responsibilities between priests and laity. This will allow the church to fulfill its mission within the unity of its body and the diversity of its members.[18]

Jacques Loew, another French Dominican, was one of the first priest-workers. He provides the perfect example of this effort to evangelise a working class milieu. He evangelised the workers and their neighborhood, and addressed their social problems through a ministry of presence, friendship, consciousness-raising, and solidarity. By the early 1950s, there were dozens of worker priests in France, a number of them belonging to the Dominican Order.

In the fall of 1953, three French Cardinals, Feltin from Paris, Gerlier from Lyons, and Liénart from Lille, went to Rome together to meet with Pope Pius XII in order to persuade him to accept this new form of ministry that they considered essential for their country's pastoral recovery. They failed to convince him. Instead, they were instructed by Rome to

18. De la Brosse, *Le Père Chenu:*, 120.

send a letter to each priest worker to inform them that the Holy Father was putting an end to this pastoral experiment.[19] From Rome's point of view, that should have been the end of the matter.

Meanwhile, however, Chenu published an article in *La Vie Intellectuelle* (1954) about the priest workers. In it, he explained that during the past ten years the French church had become sensitive to the missionary character of its new apostolic situation and to its need to evangelise 'an as yet unknown spiritual continent—the world of the worker'. The French church was in a mission context, even though it did not recognise that fact. A national church that had thought of itself as a solid Christendom eventually discovered that it had failed to enter a whole segment of the society. So now, said Chenu, the theology of the priesthood should respond to this missionary call, whether to pagan continents like China and Africa or to the new world of today's and tomorrow's industrial workers. Priestly spirituality up till now had been built upon ministry within an established Christendom. But today as in the early church, priests now have the task of evangelising a world that has never known Christ. The apostolic and pastoral authenticity of the worker priests required their entering, dwelling in, and proclaiming Christ by way of a real solidarity with the workers, even if people there are not yet ready for the preached word.[20]

While the three French cardinals and the priest workers understood Chenu perfectly, important figures in Rome considered Chenu's article an act of defiance. In reaction the Holy See took violent and abrupt measures. The Master General of the Dominicans was sent from Rome to depose the Dominican provincials of all three French provinces (Paris, Lyons, and Toulouse). As for Chenu, he and three other suspect Dominicans were silenced and exiled from Paris and from Le Saulchoir: Yves Congar, Henri Féret, and Pierre Boisselot who headed the Dominican publishing house, Les Éditions du Cerf. (Further elements of this story are told in the next chapter.) So, once more, Chenu was publicly chastised by Roman authorities who failed to understand what he represented or to respect the pastoral service that he had rendered to clergy and laity alike in awakening a missionary spirit in arthritic French Catholicism.

Exiled once again and this time forbidden to reside in Paris, Chenu was sent to the Dominican priory in Rouen, several hours distant from Paris. He reassured a friend as he was leaving, 'There's no example in his-

---

19. De la Brosse, *Le Père Chenu*, 138.
20. Chenu, 'Le Sacerdoce des Prêtres Ouvriers', 275f.

tory of any society being able to adopt important changes without first resisting them and opposing them as something that appears to upset the balance of its life'.[21] By 'society' here, Chenu meant the institutional church. To another friend he simply said, 'It'll be okay; you'll see . . . ' And once again, he obeyed.

Creative Teacher and Indefatigable Scholar

Despite all the distractions caused by his administrative duties, his editorial responsibilities, his pastoral assistance to groups and individuals, and the anguish and confusion brought about by the attacks on his work and integrity, Chenu still continued working and publishing. He remained the principal resource for the Institute of Medieval Studies in Ottawa, and he came to Paris from Rouen periodically to meet with colleagues and graduate students and to serve as chaplain to the small groups that he guided. He usually ended up consoling those who were disturbed by the measures taken against him, remaining enthusiastic, cheerful, and inspiring to others without abandoning his theological and pastoral ideas.

His growing list of publications manifested a special kind of genius not only for hard work, but particularly for an unusual type of insight that could interpret medieval texts within their historical and cultural contexts. Chenu's scholarship bridged the gap between centuries by bringing the arguments of Albert the Great, Aquinas, and other great thinkers of the twelfth and thirteenth centuries into dialogue with comparable situations in the twentieth century. As a professional historian, he was employing a prophetic charism.

Chenu's *Introduction to the Study of Saint Thomas Aquinas* was, in the words of theologian Jean-Pierre Torrell, "a book without equal, one that influenced generations of medievalists and renewed the approach that they took to Saint Thomas."[22] Chenu succeeded in doing something unprecedented by interpreting his master St Thomas through the historical, cultural, philosophical, and spiritual atmosphere of Thomas' century. Chenu recognised and explained the significance of Aquinas' cultural environment, showing how much St Thomas shared with the evangelistic spirit of St Dominic's and St Francis' mendicant movement, and how

21. De la Brosse, *Le Père Chenu,* 146.
22. Jean-Pierre Torrell, *Initiation à saint Thomas d'Aquin: sa personne et son oeuvre* (Fribourg: Editions Universitaires Fribourg, 1993), xi.

Thomas' use of Aristotle's philosophical realism led him to view Christ's Incarnation in concrete ways that had consequences for theology and the spiritual life. Chenu also showed how fully Aquinas had mastered the techniques and methodologies of the thirteenth century universities of which he was so prominent a member.

This book allowed those who would never meet Chenu in person to experience his creative and generous personality. At the end of each chapter Chenu proposed not only bibliographies for further study, but suggested areas for research. Many young scholars became genuinely excited about medieval studies in reading Chenu, and those who have carried his pioneering work forward by their own scholarship still acknowledge their enduring debt to him.

Undeterred by the punitive measures taken against him by the Vatican in the 1940s and 50s, Chenu published over the years several editions of *Theology as a Science in the Thirteenth Century* and *Theology in the Twelfth Century*. A shorter synthetic book was *St Thomas d'Aquin et la Théologie*. Some sense of Chenu's vigorous style can be grasped in the following passage from this latter work:

> You cannot share [theology's] confidence in the mystery and then be afraid of an intrusion of reason within the new synthesis ... There is a famous remark of Bonaventure, the Franciscan Master of the neighboring school next to Thomas's in Paris: he said that he was more attentive to the intrusion than to the synthesis, and recalled the dream of St. Jerome who saw himself being whipped at the last judgment for having taken pleasure in reading Cicero. Bonaventure denounced the use of philosophy in theology by many, including the Friars Preachers, saying: 'It is like mixing water in the pure wine of the Word of God.' Thomas, taking up the terms of the miracle of Cana, replied, somewhat humorously, 'It's not a case of mixing water in the wine, but of turning water into wine.'[23]

---

23. M-D Chenu, *Aquinas and His Role in Theology*, translated by Paul Philibert (Collegeville, MN: Liturgical Press, 2002), 28. This is the English translation of Chenu's *Saint Thomas d'Aquin et la théologie* (Paris: Editions du Seuil, 1959).

In addition to allowing twentieth century readers to feel a bit of the tension within which Aquinas worked, this passage also had reverberations for Chenu's personal story as well. A lot of Chenu's courage came from his intimate knowledge of and love for St Thomas. Within Chenu's writings, the thirteenth century debates at the University of Paris were being replayed with different themes in the twentieth century, and Chenu was confident that once again a reasonable faith would win in the end.

During this period of his life, Chenu was also working more fully at interpreting the significance of faith and grace in a rapidly changing culture. Chenu was confident that mature reasoning employed in the exercise of theological reflection *was* theology. An important example of this is his seminal contribution to a theology of work.[24]

Keenly aware how the working classes were alienated from the economic profit of their labor by the industrial system, Chenu undertook to address the perspective of the theological meaning of work. Even in Belgium, he had introduced the Dominican friars to the philosophy of Karl Marx and to Marx's interpretation of the alienation of workers in an industrial economy. Chenu was vividly aware of the stakes in addressing the social and economic aspects of the question. But in a creative and original approach, Chenu addressed the question of work neither from a nostalgia for an artisanal past nor from a question of personal and social justice, but from a much broader perspective. He was convinced that industrialization was creating a new type of society, what he called a civilization of work.

Chenu wanted to explain how this transformation of work affected the situation within which God's word is proclaimed and taught. The radical transformation of technology had changed social structures and created a new mentality. Theologians and preachers needed to be conscious of these changes. Chenu described this new context:

> Depersonalization is the normal effect of the shift from tools to machines, from workshop to factory, and from profession to automated labor ... In technological culture there is also an inhibition or a paralysis of the creativity in the worker; the quest for efficiency and speed is accompanied by a disdain for interiority and spiritual presence.[25]

---

24. M-D Chenu, *Pour une théologie du travail* (Paris: Editions du Seuil, 1955); English translation, *The Theology of Work*, translated by Lilian Soiron (Chicago: Regnery, 1963). See Potworowski, 127f, for a theological analysis and critique of Chenu's approach.

25. M-D Chenu, 'Théologie du travail', in *L'Évangile dans le temps*, 551.

Nonetheless Chenu sees within these undeniable tendencies hints at some possible gains for humanity.

Citing Psalm 8, 'You have made them a little lower than God, and crowned them with glory and honor. You have given them dominion over the works of your hands; you have put all things under their feet . . .' (vv 6-7), Chenu observed that what is needed is not a moralistic condemnation of the industrial system so much as a vision vast enough to provide a relevant perspective. The Scriptures show how the domination of matter has as its divinely assigned goal the development of humanity. In this context he says:

> Faced with technology that alienates workers from the economic profit of their labor and that ignores political responsibility, the violent aspirations of the underdeveloped peoples find a troubling situation. Yet within exactly this context, the masses of humanity should discover beneath their feelings of rivalry a need for solidarity, and Christians should dare to see in this critical situation fertile soil for expressing fraternal love.[26]

Work is not humanised and christianised primarily through the private intentions of the workers. The objective reality of what is being made provides the real meaning and the collective value of work. This fact must lead us to recognise that the authentic meaning of work is building the world according to God's plan. Chenu explains this point as follows:

> God did not create a ready-made universe in which he placed humans like angelic spirits in a material world, or like spectators in a landscape that is alternately enticing and crippling. God is calling human beings to be his partners in the progressive development of a universe in which they are also meant to be the image of God—God's demiurge and consciousness . . . [27]

Even though work is created by human beings, it also contributes to their humanisation. Through work, human mastery over matter is supposed to

---

26. M-D Chenu, 'Théologie du travail', 552.
27. M-D Chenu, 'Théologie du travail', 554.

open up the way to the universal cultural development of all humanity. The question of work cannot be divorced from a social vision of global human community. To achieve that goal, we need a new theology of creation. Chenu goes so far as to say that humans might be called co-creators of the universe, if the expression were not theologically so ambiguous. However, human beings are responsible now to organise and develop the nature's potential, serving as the intelligence and love that only humanity can express, and taking on responsibility to orient all these things onto the right path so as to return to their creator. Human beings, using their freedom, which is the expression of intelligence and love, become the demiurge (the divine ambassadors) of this return. In light of this, Chenu defines work as the confrontation of humanity with nature.

The religious significance of work can be found within social activities—not by imposing some devotional or moral attitude on them, but by giving them the right orientation for human action in the world.[28] In a worthy aphorism Chenu says: 'Christians no more withdraw from the spiritual life than they withdraw from the church of Jesus Christ when they become involved in creating such a world.'[29] The church follows the law of the incarnation: Jesus Christ is truly God and truly human. So it follows that the church, as the sacrament of the divine presence on earth, takes on the shape of the real human situations in which people find themselves. This is neither nostalgia for an imagined ideal past nor a pageant about paradise. People have to choose to live their lives meaningfully in light of the full significance of Christ's Incarnation. Ultimately, Chenu wanted to elevate the theology of work to a clearer level of discourse.

He repeatedly pointed out that the church had sacramentalised the human family by the sacrament of matrimony, had organised the faith communities of neighborhoods into parishes, but had always failed to become seriously invested in this other community that is the community of workers. Work is the act through which human beings are linked to nature and to the cosmos. The spirituality of workers is the investment of their spirit in the transformation of the world, and the church can no longer allow this massive reality of human society to unfold without paying attention to its biblical message about creation and justice and the destiny of humanity.

---

28. M-D Chenu, 'Théologie du travail', 557.
29. M-D Chenu, 'Théologie du travail', 563.

Dramatic Changes: A New Pope and a World-Wide Council

Pope Pius XII died in October, 1958, and was succeeded by a new pope who took the name John XXIII. He soon announced his plan for an ecumenical council to be held in Rome beginning in 1962. In this new climate, lots of things began to change. In September, 1962, Chenu was allowed to return to Paris and to live in his former priory of Saint-Jacques.[30] The role of theologians, so often treated with suspicion by the previous pope, became critically important for a church on the threshold of a council. Each bishop participating in the Second Vatican Council was allowed to bring an advisor with him as his personal theologian. So Bishop Claude Rolland of Antisirabé in Madagascar, once a student at Le Saulchoir, invited Chenu to accompany him to Rome.[31] Chenu's interests and theological activities quickly became focused on the projects of the council.

In Rome, Chenu mingled with bishops and theologians whom he had known or communicated with through the years, remaining in contact especially with Yves Congar and other Dominican experts at the council. He became involved in the seminars that theologians offered to the bishops, to the Protestant observers, and to the press. He also sent occasional articles about the council to the French weekly, *Témoignage Chrétien*. One of his most noteworthy initiatives came when Chenu conceived the idea of proposing that the council's bishops should send a message to the whole world to indicate their interest in and concern for the world. Père Congar describes this in his Council Journal:

> *September 16 or 17 (1962)*, I received from Fr Chenu the draft of a preliminary declaration. It seemed to me there and then that this initiative was *INSPIRED*, that it was *THIS* that was NEEDED! Though I did find Fr Chenu's text a little sociological, too human. Of course it is a message addressed to humankind. But I would have liked there to have been a stronger reference to the fact of Jesus Christ and the offer of the Covenant. Also, I wanted to support Fr Chenu's initiative effectively. So I sent his text, with a note of my own, to Cardinals Liénart, Alfrink, König, Döpfner, and Montini; also to Frings and Suenens [and others] . . . I received a very favorable reply from several of them, especially from Cardi-

30. De la Brosse, *Le Père Chenu,* 173.
31. De la Brosse, *Le Père Chenu,* 194.

nals Liénart, Alfrink and Döpfner. I wrote to tell Fr Chenu
what they had said. Cardinal Liénart's reply suggested that
it would be good to prepare A TEXT. Fr Chenu had drafted
one in French which I corrected and added to as regards the
paragraph concerning ecumenism, which was a little too
short as originally drafted. I typed this text and sent it to on
Küng so that he could translate it into German.[32]

Congar's collaboration and support, given his breadth of contacts with the
most prominent figures at the council, led to Chenu's initiative becoming,
after some editing by a group of bishops, the first statement of the Second
Vatican Council.[33] The council's 'Message to Humanity' was approved and
released by the council on 20 October 1962. Following Chenu's suggestion, for the first time in the history of ecumenical councils, a council of
the Roman Catholic Church addressed itself to all people throughout the
world—all of humanity—not just members of the Church. The opening
lines were: "We take great pleasure in sending to all people and nations a
message concerning that well-being, love and peace which were brought
into the world by Christ Jesus, the Son of the living God and entrusted to
the church."[34] Although Chenu complained that his original text was 'being drowned in holy water',[35] he saw a number of his perennial concerns
articulated in the message:

> Coming together in unity from every nation under the sun,
> we carry in our hearts the hardships, the bodily and mental
> distress, the sorrows, the longings and hopes of all the peo-
> ples entrusted to us. We urgently turn our thoughts to all the
> anxieties by which modern man is afflicted. Hence, let our
> concern swiftly focus first of all on those who are especially
> lowly, poor, and weak . . .[36]

---

32. Yves Congar, *My Journal of the Council*, translated by Mary John Ronanye, OP, and
Mary Cecily Boulding, OP, edited by Denis Minns OP (Adelaide: ATF Press, 2012), 81.
33. Henri Fesquet, *The Drama of Vatican II*, translated by Bernard Murchland (New York:
Random House, 1967), 29–30. See Giuseppe Alberigo and Joseph A Komonchak, editors, *History of Vatican II* (Maryknoll, NY and Leuven: Orbis and Peeters, 1997): I,
53–4.
34. *The Documents of Vatican II*, translated by Joseph Gallagher, edited by Walter M Ab-
bott (New York: Guild Press, 1966), 3.
35. Cited in *History of Vatican II*, 53.
36. *Documents of Vatican II*, 5.

In addition to his many lectures and meetings with bishops and journalists,[37] Chenu's other great contribution to Vatican II was his participation in the commission writing Schema XIII, ultimately to become *Gaudium et Spes*, the Constitution on the Church in the Modern World. In that council document, Chenu (like Lebret) saw several of his lifelong theological convictions enter into the church's official teaching. The theme of the 'signs of the times', long a favorite idea of Chenu's, became integrated into the constitution's framework, as did the idea that church and society mutually give and take resources and strengths from one another for the benefit of humanity. Chenu's phrase, already notable in the 'Message to Humanity', that the joys, hopes, griefs and anxieties of all humanity are those of the church, became the leitmotif of the whole document in its first paragraph. For the rest of his days, Chenu rejoiced in the council's adoption of this pastoral constitution and delighted to remember his role in helping it to shape it.

Chenu had come to understand that the locus of theology, the place where theological reflection emerges, is the convergence between the living faith of believers and their confrontation with the changing world. The experience of being a Christian is an inexhaustible source for understanding the sacred tradition constituted by God's word as received by the church's magisterium and its theologians. The world and the church's life are not just 'problems', but also resources for theologians. There will always be the challenge to understand them, to make sense of them in the light of Christ who is God and man, spirit and flesh, divine and human, eternal and historical. In an essay on the 'pastoral' character of the council, Chenu wrote that:

> When the council was given the task of finding a language to announce the Good News to the world, it was not only a question of the art with which it used words, images, symbols and forms suited to twentieth-century people, as if putting new clothes on an old teaching. What matters is the communication of God's word as a kind of dialogue with people through and in a church that understands itself to be missionary. God's word speaks today.[38]

---

37. Historian Jan Grootaers notes, in *History of Vatican II*, 526: 'Among the foreign theologians who quickly acquired an extraordinary influence on the Italian laity I must mention at least Father M.-D. Chenu, who always made himself available to informal groups and had a gift for friendly encounters.'
38. M-D Chenu, 'Un Concile "Pastoral"', in *L'Evangile dans le Temps*, 663.

Any artificial division between the pastoral and the doctrinal is a mistake.

> 'Doctrine' will rob evangelization of its energy if it is imag-
> ined to be abstract principles out of touch with a changing
> world. History is part of the fabric of the kingdom of God
> and of the pilgrim church on its way to its full realization.
> Tradition can't be thought of as an inventory of propositions
> bundled into a book of dogmas.[39] Pastoral teaching is doc-
> trine that has found a way to become incarnated in the lives
> of believers. Vatican II was simultaneously pastoral, ecumen-
> ical, concerned about the world, committed to the poor, and
> sensitive to the dramatic issues of the surrounding world by
> virtue of the message it was given to proclaim.[40]

The Legacy of a Challenging Life

Chenu spoke with a unique and intrepid voice in a church that was on
the defensive and troubled by the shock waves of two world wars, leaking
communicants like a rusty barrel and fearful of Marxist socialism and secular humanism. He was convinced that the institutional church was made
for people, not people for the church. He always used the test of freedom –
spontaneity, deep investment, delight—as an indicator of authentic gospel
living. Because of the clarity of his perspective and the authenticity of his
instincts, he spent a lifetime recruiting people to freedom and creativity,
including theologians, historians, lay apostles, even bishops.

I asked a friar who was close to Chenu at the Priory of Saint-Jacques if
he could sum up Chenu's influence on his Dominican brothers in his last
years. His gave me a touching description of Chenu's character. 'When
people found themselves with Père Chenu, they immediately felt better',
he wrote, 'even if Chenu hadn't yet spoken a word to them. Persons who
have that kind of uplifting influence are extremely rare, but he was one of
them.' Then he added an interesting anecdote: 'Chenu was encouragement
itself. He would often take notes in the midst of a conversation with you
and if you appeared amazed, he would say, "Go on, little brother, what
you're saying really interests me; this is even better than what you said last
time." He was genuinely interested and was on the lookout for some new
source of hope to *the very end*.'

---

39. M-D Chenu, 'Un Concile "Pastoral"', 666.
40. M-D Chenu, 'Un Concile "Pastoral"', 672.

Chenu's life helps us to understand Vatican II better. Chenu lived through some of the worst moments of the subtle ecclesiastical totalitarianism of the papacy of Pope Pius XII and yet he never ceased to believe in a better day. His powerful sense of history made him realise that the present shell of evolving ecclesiastical structures can never do justice to nor can they ultimately destroy the divine treasure that they carry within. Further, Chenu was himself a grace for the church. He made countless converts to a graced optimism in the face of terrible disappointments.

If he was a master of theology, he was first and foremost a master of humanity. As his younger Dominican colleague Claude Geffré admiringly wrote of him: 'Rarely did one man succeed so well at mastering intellectual rigor, affectionate attention to other persons, and wise discernment about down to earth reality.'[41] At his death, tributes came from the hierarchy, from theologians, historians and other academics, from clerical and lay pastoral leaders, and from his Dominican brothers and sisters as well. All felt close to him.

After his death, I found among his papers these notes he wrote for his Prayers of the Faithful for the Feast of Pentecost. They say a lot about him:

- That we can recognise the presence of the Holy Spirit in the events of world history . . .
- That we may bear witness to Christ's message by the boldness of our decisions with the light and in the freedom of the Spirit . . .
- That the world's transformations may be opportune moments for the ecclesial community to bring about its fuller incarnation in society . . .
- For clergy and laity alike, that we may know how to recognise the functions and ministries to which our lives are calling us, so that the Spirit will renew the face of the earth through us, let us pray to the Lord.

Lord, give us the insight and the boldness not to be afraid when faced with great changes in our world, but rather to see your creation at work in them. Through these changes and the gift of the Holy Spirit, may we become your partners. Amen.

---

41. Claude Geffré, *Passion de l'Homme, Passion de Dieu* (Paris: Editions du Cerf, 1991), 245.

Père Chenu died on 11 February 1990, at the age of ninety-five. In an obituary in the Paris daily *Le Monde*, Jean-Pierre Jossua wrote: 'The French Dominicans owe him so much of the splendid vitality of this period of their lives, and so does the church—much more than it has ever been willing to acknowledge.'[42]

---

42. Jean-Pierre Jossua, "La Mort du Père Marie-Dominique Chenu: un théologien libre et engagé," *Le Monde*, Feb. 13, 1990.

Chapter 3

Yves Congar: Scholar and Pioneer

Often the French Dominicans who were important in the life of the Catholic Church in the twentieth century made contributions to more than one area of church life. Yves Congar joined research in the history of the forms of the church to an advocacy of the ecumenical movement for Christian unity. He was a comprehensive theoretician of tradition as well as a pastoral theologian of the local church. Richard McBrien wrote: 'By any reasonable account, Yves Congar is the most distinguished ecclesiologist of this century and perhaps of the entire post-Tridentine era. No modern theologian's spirit was accorded fuller play in the documents of Vatican II than Congar's.'[1]

Life and Work

Congar was born on 13 April 1904, in Sedan, France into a family originally from Celtic Brittany. After a few years at a seminary attached to the Institut Catholique in Paris that initiated him into the thought of Thomas Aquinas, he entered the Dominicans of the Province of France in 1925.

---

1. Richard P McBrien, 'Church and Ministry: The Achievement of Yves Congar', in *Theology Digest* 32 (1985): 203. Frère Émile, de Taizé, *Fidèle à l'avenir. À l'Écoute du Cardinal Congar* (Taizé: Les Presses de Taizé, 2011); Anthony Oelrich, *A Church Fully Engaged: Yves Congar's Vision of Ecclesial Authority* (Collegeville: Liturgical Press, 2011); Elizabeth Teresa Groppe, *Yves Congar's Theology of the Holy Spirit* (New York: Oxford University Press, 2004); Joseph Famerée, *L'Écclésiologie d'Yves Congar* (Louvain: Leuven University Press, 1992); *Yves Congar* (Paris: Cerf, 2008); Cornelis ThM van Vliet, *Communio sacramentalis: Das Kirchenverständnis von Yves Congar—genetisch und systematisch betrachtet* (Mainz: Matthias-Grünewald, 1995); Thomas F O'Meara, 'Reflections on Yves Congar and Theology in the United States', in *US Catholic Historian* 17 (1999): 91–105; Jean-Pierre Jossua, *La Théologie au service du peuple de Dieu* (Paris: Cerf, 1967), 25—English translation: *Yves Congar: Theology in the Service of God's People* (Dubuque: The Priory Press, 1968).

Congar's studies were at the Dominican school in exile, Le Saulchoir near Tournai, Belgium. Étienne Fouilloux observes: 'Yves Congar was one of the young intellectuals who, in the quieter circumstances after World War I, turned from the secular clergy to the more prestigious orders or congregations, particularly the Preaching Friars and the Society of Jesus. Vocations among them reached an unexpected high-water mark: twenty four novices in his class among whom were close friends and a few future celebrities like the artist Marie-Alain Couturier, the philosopher Domi-nique Dubarle, and the editor and publisher Augustin-Jean Maydieu.'[2] At the Dominican studium the theologian A-G Sertillanges, the historian Pierre Mandonnet, and the philosopher Ambroise Gardeil were inspiring depth and creativity in that remarkable group of younger Dominicans. M-D Chenu, knowledgeable in the intellectual and cultural history of the Middle Ages, offered an insightful and systematic exposition of Aquinas' theology at the center of a school studying and encouraging intellectual diversity. 'The house of studies was for Congar the framework of a basic encounter: not with an academic discipline but with a man only twelve years older, the young and dynamic Fr Chenu. His course on the his-tory of Christian doctrines ended with the theological school of Tübin-gen and the recent meetings of the ecumenical movement.'[3] The faculty developed their own approach to theological education, deeply histori-cal and intensely contemporary. They offered the ideas of great Christian theologians in the context of their historical periods but in dialogue with contemporary issues.

As the young Dominican finished his seminary studies, he decided that his vocation was to be in theology, but in a theology aiming at church unity. His particular theological approach was not to be philosophical but historical; he would research the history of the forms of the church in its various periods. This knowledge would serve church renewal and ecu-menical dialogue. 'I knew very early what I wanted to do. This is how it happened. I was a student at Le Saulchoir, ordained to the priesthood on the feast of St James (25 July 1930). To prepare myself for ordination, I made a special study of the Gospel according to John, and read along with

---

2.   Fouilloux, 'Friar Yves, Cardinal Congar, Dominican: Itinerary of a Theologian', in *US Catholic Historian* 17 (1999): 67; Congar, 'La route devant moi: premiers pas', in *Écrits réformateurs* (Paris: Cerf, 1995), 267–301.
3.   Fouilloux, 'Un théologien dans l'Église du XXe siècle', in *Bulletin de littérature ecclési-astique* 106 (2005): 25; Fergus Kerr, 'Yves Congar and Thomism', in *Yves Congar: Theo-logian of the Church*, edited by Gabriel Flynn (Grand Rapids: Eerdmans, 2005), 67–97.

it the commentary of Thomas Aquinas. I was deeply moved, overwhelmed by chapter 17; this is sometimes called "the priestly prayer" but I prefer to call it "the apostolic prayer of Jesus on Christian unity".[4] After 1931 he taught ecclesiology as part of a new team at the Dominican studium; then Le Saulchoir moved to a location outside Paris in 1937.

Catholics and the Ecumenical Movement

Congar's superiors approved his desire to work in the new area of ecumenism. 'I had often expressed to my superiors the desire to work for unity, a desire which would mean working predominantly among Protestants. My superiors never opposed this or even raised objections, although sometimes I had the feeling that one or another rather questioned the usefulness of all this.'[5] He visited Germany several times in the 1930s. The young theologian knew that historical research and ecumenical meetings required knowledge of German, and he also felt a need to visit the places associated with Martin Luther.[6]

He published in periodicals surveys of books and articles from around Europe on ecumenism, ecclesiology, and the history of theology; and part of his success as a historian and ecclesiologist came from those detailed surveys of ideas and literature drawn up from 1931 to 1977.[7] In 1932, he asked whether the twentieth century was in a particular way a century of the church. If so, was this age urging renewal upon the church? In 1935 he published in *La Vie Intellectuelle* a long article exploring reasons for non-belief in modern times. Christians are presenting to others a largely diluted faith, one that is not sufficiently incarnational and human. That faith is too linked to the institution of the church where hierarchical leadership is disciplining and silencing people rather than enhancing their ministries.[8]

---

4. 'Letter from Yves Congar, OP', in *Theology Digest* 32 (1985): 213.
5. Congar, *Une Passion: l'unité* (Paris: Cerf, 1974), 14.
6. 'I had an intimation that there was something profound to discover and understand in Luther. At Le Saulchoir there was an interest in Luther—and in a way different from that of Grisar or Denifle . . . I visited the great Lutheran sites . . . and gained access to original documents' ('Appels et Cheminements 1929-1963', in *Écrits réformateurs*, 268).
7. Jean-Marie Vezin, 'Yves Congar, rédacteur de bulletins: un aspect de l'oeuvre', in *Revue des sciences philosophiques et théologiques* 92 (2008): 601–621; see Michael Quisinsky, 'Congar avec Chenu et Féret au Saulchoir des années 1930', [catho-theo.net] [Freiburg im. Br.].
8. Congar, 'Une Conclusion théologique à l'enquête sur les raisons actuelles de l'incroyance', in *La Vie intellectuelle* 37 (1935): 214–259.

After 1932, he spoke to countless meetings of people—groups of pastors or small gatherings of Catholics and Protestants—and explained the idea of cooperation among churches. He attended the pioneering meetings of *Life and Work* at Oxford and Edinburgh after 1937, where he met men who were to be the leaders of various Protestant churches and of the future World Council of Churches. A friend had begun a yearly ecumenical event called the Week of Christian Unity, days of prayer and preaching, to be held in January between the feasts of St Peter and St Paul. He preached during that week of prayer for unity every year from 1936 to 1964—in Europe but also in the Middle East. In 1936 Congar's series of sermons on ecumenism at Sacré Coeur drew considerable attention. (During one of those sermons his neurological illness made a first appearance in a slight numbness in his arm). The ideas given in talks and sermons were drawn into the book *Divided Christendom* published in 1937. That was one of the first Roman Catholic books on ecumenism and also the first title in Congar's collection of studies in ecclesiology. That series *Unam Sanctam* became over the years a prestigious assembly of eighty volumes (including twenty books of commentaries on the documents of Vatican II).

Congar was a prolific writer. In one year, 1937, the book on Catholic ecumenism appeared as well as articles on the theology of mysticism, characteristics of Catholicism and Protestantism, Thomas Aquinas and truth, the Dominican Louis Chardon who wrote on Baroque spirituality, recent ecumenical conferences, and the uncertain value of private revelations. Theology was to be a vital catalyst for change in human society and in the church: 'To every growth of humanity . . . there should correspond a growth of the church, an incorporation of the faith, an incarnation of grace, a humanization of God! That is the church. That is Catholicism.'[9] In September of 1930, a few weeks after his ordination, he had composed in Düsseldorf a prayer about the frozen state of the church at that time

> God, why does your church always condemn? True she must guard the deposit of faith, but is there no other means but condemnation? . . . If your church were only more encouraging, more comprehensive . . . . The church must make itself intelligible to every human ear . . . The times press—there is so much work to be done.[10]

---

9. Jossua, *La Théologie au service du peuple de Dieu*, 25.

10. Congar, *Dialogue between Christians* (Westminster: Newman, 1966), 5–7; see Alberic Stacpoole, 'Early Ecumenism, Early Congar, 1904-1940', in *The Month* 259 (January, 1988): 502–10.

Nazi Germany was seeking to conquer Europe. Congar was drafted in 1939 into military service (French priests and religious were not exempt), and was captured in 1940. He tried to escape five times, ending up after 1941 in maximum security prisons. 'My friendships in the camp of Colditz and then of Lübeck have been one of the three great graces of my life.'[11] Congar regretted how war and prison had cost him years of research and work.[12] At the beginning of 1942 in a prisoner of war camp he learned that a book by his mentor Chenu, describing the historical context of the theology presented at the Le Saulchoir, had just been placed on *The Index of Forbidden Books* by the Vatican. Chenu was removed from the faculty. His error was advocating the study of theology from a historical perspective; that implied that the human personality, philosophy, and Christian theology are not everywhere one and timeless.

After the War, working in the history of ecclesiology, Congar tirelessly researched how various concrete forms had entered and served the life of the church in different times and cultures. He was particularly attentive to German theological literature, which was not widely accessible. His many summaries of theological literature reach their climax in the magisterial survey of ecclesiology from St Augustine to after Vatican II published in 1970 and in the two volumes of the theologies of tradition born of history. Teaching at Le Saulchoir from 1950 to 1954, he wrote on ecumenism, the laity, Orthodox ecclesiology, and the theology of the biblical and preached word. He worked with the many men and women in France who were involved in a renewal of the liturgy, religious education, and preparation for reception of the sacraments.

> Anyone who did not live during the years of French Catholicism after the war missed one of the finest movements in the life of the church. Through a slow emergence from misery, one tried in the great freedom of a fidelity as profound as life to rejoin in a Gospel way the world, a world of which the

---

11. Jean-Pierre Jossua, 'Yves Congar: Un Portrait', in *Études* 384 (September, 1995): 212.
12. 'Faithful among the faithful, Congar, although overextended by multiple tasks, admired his fellow prisoners and he did not hesitate to take the time to write in 1948 *Leur Résistance: Mémorial des officiers évadés, anciens de Colditz et de Lübeck*. His companions repaid him: in the mail which he received after his removal from the Saulchoir in 1954 many of the former prisoners of war manifested their support and often their puzzlement. These solid friendships did not compensate for the break in his momentum caused by those years of forced quasi-inactivity' (Fouilloux, 'Friar Yves, Cardinal Congar, Dominican', 73).

church could become an integral part for the first time in centuries.[13]

He published a study of reform in the church through the centuries, *True and False Reform*.[14] There were also books on the identity of the priest and the roles of the baptised in the local church and on how the underlying principle of incarnation is present in Christ, Mary, and the church. The nine hundredth anniversary of the schism between the Eastern and Western Churches occasioned a study of the collegial and local aspects of Orthodox ecclesiology. Essays treating salvation outside the church—even grace for those living on other planets—were gathered into *Wide World, My Parish: Salvation and Its Problems*.[15]

Criticisms from the Vatican followed upon the publication of each of those important books, some of which were not permitted to receive second printings. From 1939 on, the Vatican informed the superior of the Dominicans that these studies on church and ecumenism had serious errors. Congar was brought to Rome for examinations, that then never took place. 'The censors are not happy with me and they don't like my approach because (1) I work in new areas, on the frontiers, and (2) my efforts result in questioning and challenging their theology.'[16] In October, 1953, Cardinal Pizzardo, director of the Holy Office (formerly the Inquisition) wrote to the head of the Dominicans Emmanuel Suarez: 'You know well the new ideas and tendencies, not only exaggerated but even erroneous,

---

13. *Dialogue between Christians*, 32.
14. A translation in English by Paul Philibert has appeared: *True and False Reform in the Church* (Collegeville: Liturgical Press, 2010). Looking back Congar wrote: 'The manuscript of *Jalons pour une théologie du laïcat* sent to Rome was returned without prohibition . . . but other writings did not escape the pincers of Roman censure, becoming ever more malicious and strict after February, 1954' ('Appels et Cheminements 1929–1963', in *Écrits réformateurs*, 300).
15. *The Wide World My Parish: Salvation and its Problems* (Baltimore: Helicon, 1961); see the new French edition with an 'Introduction' by JMR Tillard, *Vaste monde ma paroisse* (Paris: Cerf, 2000); Thomas F O'Meara, 'Yves Congar, Theologian of Grace in a Vast World', in Gabriel Flynn, editor, *Yves Congar: Theologian of the Church* (Grand Rapids: Eerdmans, 2005), 371–400.
16. Congar's diary for October 23, 1952 cited in Fouilloux, 'Friar Yves, Cardinal Congar, Dominican', 89: 'The tragedy of the present situation and of the way in which the Roman ordinary magisterium exercises its function concretely is that this magisterium is incessantly doing theology and giving voice to the positions of a particular theological school with the authority of the Catholic magisterium'.

that are developing in the realms of theology, canon law, and society, ideas finding a considerable resonance in certain religious orders ... So-called theologians "with brilliant phrases and generalizations" teach falsehood.'[17] Suarez flew to Paris and removed from office the three French provincials and the provincial directors of studies; some professors of theology were forbidden to teach. The Vatican sought to control what many Dominicans could publish. The Paris newspaper *Le Monde* called it 'a raid on the Dominicans'. The Roman action was in strong opposition to the Dominican tradition of democracy in the selection of superiors. 'There are people who accuse us of modernism. That's unjust and libelous. They have no sense of history.'[18] Congar once observed that the Vatican's Holy Office resembled the KGB and the Nazi Gestapo: he knew this, he said, because he had had contact with two of the three. From 1954 to 1956, he lived at times in exile, in Great Britain and Jerusalem; he was limited in the topics for the articles and books he could write and had little if any public ministry. The Bishop of Strasbourg invited him in 1956 to come to the Dominican priory there. He gave occasional lectures at the university and conferences to groups on ecumenism; the Dominican community elected him prior. Then in 1960, Pope John XXIII named him a consulter for the coming ecumenical council, Vatican II.

An Ecumenical Council

We have the diaries written by Congar during his years at Vatican II. He arrived at the council wounded by years of attacks on his view of the church,

17. Cited in François Leprieur, *Quand Rome condamne* (Paris: Cerf, 1989), 42–45; see Thomas O'Meara, 'Raid on the Dominicans: The Repression of 1954', in *America* 170 (1994): 8–16.

18. Jean-M Le Guillou, 'Yves Congar', in H Vorgrimler, editor, *Bahnbrechende Theologen: Bilanz der Theologie im 20 Jh.* (Freiburg: Herder, 1970), 10. Congar wrote to his mother at that time: 'What I am blamed for is usually very little. Most of the time, whatever problem is raised about an idea in my work is explained in the preceding line in that same work. What has put me in the wrong (in their eyes) is not having said false things, but having said things they do not want to be said' (Étienne Fouilloux, 'Lettre du Père Congar à sa mère', in *La Vie spirituelle* 154 [2000]: 137). 'There are two completely different levels in intellectual and spiritual life [in the church]. For Rome a knowledge of the Gospel is essentially foreign; for us, it is the main concern ... Rome is not capable of asking itself whether Rome's positions are correct from a Christian point of view' (Congar, *Journal d'un Théologien, 1946–1958* [Paris Cerf, 2001], 251); see Johannes Bunnenberg, 'In den Fängen des Hl Offiziums. "Die düsteren Jahre" des Dominikaners Yves Congar', in *Wort und Antwort* 44 (2003): 19–24.

a figure still under suspicion. Despite the opposition of theologians like Sebastian Tromp and the pessimism of Henri de Lubac, he sensed that the council was producing its own dynamic, its own force for the Church, 'a pastoral climate, a climate of freedom and dialogue and openness'.[19] If during preliminary meetings he was uncertain, the progress of the council soon drew him into its optimistic atmosphere of renewal. There was an enormous amount of work for him to do in the commissions preparing conciliar texts. (He spoke of drafts of documents appearing in numbers like the autumn leaves falling down from the trees). To certain texts he gave their basic directions, like those on ecumenism and tradition, while for others he added important insights.[20] An entry towards the end of the council, for 7 December 1965, reveals his work and influence. 'I left slowly and with difficulty, barely able to stand. A great many bishops congratulated me, thanked me. To a good extent, it was my work, they said. Looking at things objectively, I did a great deal to prepare for the council, elaborating and diffusing ideas that the council consecrated. At the council itself, I did a great deal of work.'

He had contributed significantly to a number of texts being given final approval by the council on that day in December: the Constitutions on the Church and on Revelation, the introduction and the conclusion of the Decree on Ecumenism and the Declaration on Non-Christian Religions, sections of texts on foreign missions and on priests as well as the introduction and theological part of the Declaration on Religious Freedom. 'Thus what was read out this morning came, to a very large extent, from me.'[21] Congar saw the council as a beginning and he expected further developments and deeper reforms to occur. The upheavals that arrived in the post-conciliar era were long overdue, he observed, and their roots lay not in Vatican II but in the constrictive decades, and even centuries, before it.

His neurological illness made his work at the council difficult and by the late 1960s he was often in a wheelchair. In 1984, he moved from Saint-Jacques to the military hospital of Les Invalides. He was unable to experience directly the renewal of ministry and church around the world where his theological principles remained influential. He died on June 22, 1995.

---

19. Yves Congar, *My Journal of the Council*, translated by Mary John Ronanye, OP, and Mary Cecily Boulding, OP, edited by Denis Minns OP (Adelaide: ATF Press, 2012), 145.
20. Étienne Fouilloux, 'Un théologien dans l'Église du XXe siècle', 36.
21. Congar, *My Journal of the Council*, 870–871; see Alberto Melloni, 'The System and the Truth in the Diaries of Yves Congar', in *Yves Congar: Theologian of the Church* (Grand Rapids: Eerdmans, 2005), 277–302.

Beyond the Baroque to a Church of Service

During the council Congar wrote a small book, *Power and Poverty in the Church*.[22] The book's theme was the appearance and the reality of power in church authority and the tension between evangelical poverty and church trappings like Baroque vestments, rings, and antique fans. A first section on hierarchy as service looked at authority as it is criticised and presented in the New Testament. Jesus and Paul offer forms suited to a Christian theology of community where leadership would emerge as service. A second part looks at titles and honors in the church, considering them in their historical origins. Ideologies of authority find statement and support in clothes, symbols, and titles. Congar's book is an exposé of church hierarchy as power and display and a rejection of the voice and activity of the baptised. The critique is still relevant today.

Related to that book was his conviction that the Roman Catholic Church had retained too many forms of authority from the age of the Baroque, from that important but antiquated time of the seventeenth century. 'In ecclesiology the "theology of the Baroque" . . . insists repeatedly on the aspect of hierarchy. It situates the pope at the top of a pyramidical vision in a spirit that is a little militaristic.'[23] The Council of Trent and the subsequent Baroque, spotlighting dramatic devotions and rituals in worship and art, formed the church for centuries. 'Tridentinism . . . was a system which absorbed absolutely everything: theology, ethics, Christian behavior, religious practices, liturgy, organization, Roman centralisation, the perpetual intervention of Roman congregations in the life of the church, and so on.'[24] The church appeared as a pyramid with a small pinnacle of leadership determining everything for its many passive adherents. 'Church leadership favored the construction of a hierarchical order: not one arranged around the Eucharist but one where the "regime" of Rome occupies the center and summit.'[25] That age was restored and cultivated anew from 1840 to 1960. In the nineteenth and twentieth centuries the church, drawing on Neo-Platonic, imperial, feudal, and Baroque structures, ended in an individual, the pope, who had unlimited, oppressive authority. 'What is the situation since Vatican II with regard to the almost obsessive dominance

---

22. (Paris: Cerf, 1963).
23. Puyo, *Jean Puyo interroge le Père Congar. 'Une Vie pour la vérité'* (Paris: Le Centurion, 1975), 47.
24. 'Vatican II: Departure from Tridentinism', in *Fifty Years of Catholic Theology: Conversations with Yves Congar*, with Bernard Lauret (London: SCM Press, 1988), 3f.
25. Congar, *L'Église de Saint Augustin à l'époque moderne* (Paris: Cerf, 1970), 368.

of the Roman pontiff in classical ecclesiology? Neither the council nor the work done after the council has succeeded in reducing the authority of the pope.'[26] Then ecclesiology in its social and political structure was little more than a 'hierarchology'. From 1600 to Vatican II, as Congar observed ironically, 'the church was seen and defined not as an organism enlivened by the Holy Spirit but as an organization in which Christ had intervened in the beginning as the founder. Then the Holy Spirit gave and guaranteed authority. These two, having once given to the institution a super-terrestrial quality, would not intervene any more'.[27]

The worldwide church must pass beyond the hierarchology where only the pope and his Vatican assistants are permitted to speak and act. The churches of the New Testament and the forms of authority through the centuries inspire the alternative that is being born in the course of the twentieth century: they draw on biblical and patristic themes like the Body of Christ and the People of God. 'In leaving the Middle Ages and the Counter-Reformation we are leaving a legalism that has surrounded our ways of thinking since the end of the twelfth century. The consciousness of the church as it unfolds from the council gives a primacy to the ontology of grace over the structures of administration. After all, those structures are in place only as ministers at the service of a supernatural reality which is basically sacramental.'[28] The ministry of teaching, the magisterium, is broader than the papacy, and living tradition is richer than ancient texts. History will not let the church remain feudal and Baroque. The church is sacrament and leaven within the rest of the world, a world that is not purely temporal or secular.

> The Spirit creates from within the unity of the community and creates too the organs or expressions of its special genius, i.e., its tradition. The heart of these theological perspectives is the identity of the principle which acts throughout the church's duration, and is at work in the activities by which it builds itself up with that principle which was at work from

---

26. Congar, 'Moving towards a Pilgrim Church', in Alberic Stacpoole, editor, *Vatican II Revisited by Those Who Were There* (Minneapolis: Winston, 1986), 141.

27. *L'Église de Saint Augustin*, 386. Bernard Sesboüé surveys the observations in Congar's diary of the years of Vatican II in terms of his struggles with the *Curia Romana* ('Un Dur Combat pour une Église Conciliaire: *Mon Journal du concile* de Yves Congar', in *Revue des sciences religieuses* 91 (2003): 265–67.

28. Congar, 'L'Avenir de l'église', in *Écrits réformateurs*, 367; Congar, 'Moving towards a Pilgrim Church', 146.

beginning in the revelation made to the prophets and the apostles, and at work in the saving actions of the incarnate Word.[29]

The critique of externals and of political structures in the hierarchy flowed from and led back to a deeper theology, a view of the life and activity of the entire church as an organism animated by the Holy Spirit.

Church Life and Ministry

The church is composed of men and women led by the Spirit to charisms and ministries, movements and activities. Presented in many articles and books, Congar's ecclesiology of the church as a pneumatic community drew on St. Paul, Greek theologians and the Romantic Idealist theologian of Tübingen, Johann Adam Möhler in the nineteenth century.[30] Möhler saw the church as a living body, an organism animated by the Holy Spirit; while that perspective came from the fathers of the church, it had resonated with the philosophy of Schelling after 1800.

A book on the laity from 1953 was something new: a move away from the passivity and secularity in which church authority had placed the baptised. Were not activities manifestations of the life of the baptised in the church?[31] In the 1970s, however, he looked back at that book and saw that something further was needed: a new model for an active church with various ministers and ministries.[32]

---

29. *Tradition and Traditions: An Historical and Theological Essay* (New York: Macmillan, 1966), 340. In the 1920s, Joseph Cardijn, a Belgian diocesan priest, founded a Catholic Action movement named the 'Young Christian Workers' to encourage its lay members to understand the workplace as a field of evangelisation. Cardijn and the group's leaders frequently came to the Dominican House of Studies, Le Saulchoir (then in Belgium) for retreats and study sessions, and so the French Dominicans like Chenu, Congar and others became familiar with the YCW and it influenced their mission. It represented a creative expression of what Pope Pius XI had called 'Catholic Action'.
30. O'Meara, 'Beyond "Hierarchology": Johann Adam Möhler and Yves Congar', in Donald J Dietrich and Michael J Himes, editors, *The Legacy of the Tübingen School: The Relevance of Nineteenth-Century Theology for the Twenty-First Century* (New York: Crossroad, 1997), 173–91.
31. *Jalons pour une théologie du laïcat* (Paris: Cerf, 1953), 68f. The Vatican's Nuncio in Paris, Roncalli, read and annotated *Vraie et fausse réforme*; the spirit in those pages would lead him to the Council: Jossua, 'Yves Congar: la vie et l'oeuvre d'un théologien', in *Cristianesimo nella Storia* 17 (1996): 5.
32. Congar, 'My Path-Findings in the Theology of the Laity and Ministries', in *The Jurist* 32 (1972): 169–188. On Congar's development over decades see Hervé Legrand, 'Yves Congar (1904–1995): Une Passion pour l'unité', in *Nouvelle revue théologique*

I think the church today, particularly at the pastoral level (perhaps less in theology) is in an extraordinary phase of vitality and creativity . . . Clearly there are many new things. What I wrote on the laity in the church in 1953 is long passé. Now the laity are pressed to take over many roles in the church because there are fewer priests (many are old and few are young, an important problem in France) and, second, because the laity are more conscious of the character of baptism. Baptism makes them to be active members of the mystical body of Christ . . . Laypeople do not replace priests; there will always be priests in the church. But the laity can and must at times lead the community, pray, and explain the Word of God. This is true for women as well as men. The role of women is extremely important not just because they are often involved in the church greater numbers.[33]

His theology of ministry suggests an image of concentric circles. There are a number of ministries and ministers; they are not the same; pastor and bishop are the leaders and center, although readers, educators, ministers to the sick, and liturgists are truly in the church's public ministry. This is the reality of the diocese and parish today. The Spirit is the underlying vivifying force of diversity and participation. When Karl Barth asked Congar about the essential idea of the council, he replied, 'service, the animation of ministries'.[34]

After 1985, more and more isolated by his illness, Congar had little contact with the expansion of church ministry around the world apart from what he read. 'There have been many contemporary developments in the life of the church . . . The laity often take initiatives that are very much in the spirit of the Gospel. I have often said, and I must say it again, that we are in one of the most evangelistic centuries of all of history.'[35]

126 (2004): 529–54 and Joseph Famerée, 'Aux Origines de Vatican II: La démarche théologique d'Yves Congar', in *Ephemerides Theologicae Lovanienses* 61 (1995): 122–33.

33. Frano Prcela, OP, 'Pionier der kirchlichen Erneuerung: Yves Congar OP (13: 4. 1904-22: 6. 1995)', in *Wort und Antwort* 36 (1995): 130, 133. Congar continued to write in the 1970s: for instance, *I Believe in the Holy Spirit*, 3 volumes (New York: Seabury, 1983) and the essays in *Église et papauté* (Paris: Cerf, 1994).

34. *Fifty Years of Catholic Theology: Conversations with Yves Congar,* 57; see A Nisus, 'Genèse d'une ecclésiologie de communion dans l'oeuvre d'Y. Congar', in *Revue des sciences philosophiques et théologiques* 94 (2010): 309–334.

35. A Nisus, 'Genèse d'une ecclésiologie', 66.

Thinking about the Gospel

In an organic communion vitalised by the Spirit, the baptised—teachers, theologians, and activists—should have their voice in pondering revelation. 'The magisterium must not be isolated from the living reality of the church. The originality of the theologians' charism and service must be recognised. Their work should be carried out in communion with the concrete lives of the faithful, in the context of the liturgy, and in an atmosphere of discussion. Theologians are not to be regarded only from the point of view of a dependence on Rome.' It was time for a reversal inspired by the ecclesiologies of the early Christian communities. 'One must put at the top truth, the apostolic faith that has been handed down, confessed, preached, and celebrated. Under it, at its service, we place the magisterial reality, an apostolic ministry along with the research and teaching of theologians along with the faith of the baptised.'[36]

Tradition and Traditions analyses the many relationships of the bishop of Rome to other people in the church in terms of all of them reflecting on the Gospel. 'A treatise on tradition that ignored God's continuous inspiration of the Church would be utterly useless. Such a divine action is constitutive of Tradition.'[37] The book, outlining different kinds of teaching, presents the reality of tradition first in history and then in systematic theology. Today's existential challenge to the church is, as Vatican II showed, to accept history.

> Everything is absolutely historical including the person of Jesus Christ. The Gospel is historical; Thomas Aquinas is historical; Pope Paul VI is historical. Note that historical does not mean just that Jesus came at a certain point in time but that one must draw the consequences of this fact, that he lives on through temporality. He develops like every other man; his consciousness grows, his knowledge expands.[38]

---

36. Congar, 'Bref Historique des Formes du 'Magistère' et de ses relations avec les docteurs', in *Revue des sciences philosophiques et théologiques* 60 (1976): 112.
37. *Tradition and Traditions: An Historical and Theological Essay*, 452. 'Tradition is ultimately synthetic in its manner of growth: it contains documents and objective facts, original data and life, all given through the Holy Spirit, an objective external norm together with a living subject' (*Tradition and Traditions*, 458).
38. *Jean Puyo interroge le Père Congar*, 43. 'A better knowledge of history and of historical conditions to which is added the sociology of knowledge is important . . . History does not just make us assistants at a sequence of re-readings. At the level of formulation and

Moreover, not just the papacy but other pneumatic services in the church have important roles in interpreting the Gospel anew. 'The monarchical theory, according to which everything depends on one (*monos*) who communicates his power to all the bishops, was still held at Vatican II, by Fr Gagnebet and many others. But this theory cannot be sustained. It is *historically* indefensible.'[39]

Tradition is a historical and communal reality coming from a presence of the Holy Spirit in the varied Body of Christ. Tradition is much more than historical documents or the Vatican administration: it is the ongoing life of the whole church. The Catholic Church is rediscovering itself as the People of God made up of all Christians. The church is not a juridical organization but a social group whose forms come from and flow into history; all the members have powers to let the institution expand in the world in which the church exists and to which it is sent.[40]

***

Yves Congar was a particularly influential Catholic theologian in the twentieth century. Jean-Pierre Jossua describes him as 'a figure emblematic of the theology of the council, perhaps the most known theologian of the century'.[41] He was creative by the time he was thirty; the agenda and the event of Vatican II was partly the effort and goal of his writings. Joseph Famerée summed this up:

> The originality of the ecclesiology of Congar looked at as a totality flows from the individuality of his personal journey. Three areas strike us: a precise awakening in the life of the church and the theology of the church; a rather new method in the theology of the church which includes the life of the church; solidly researched teaching including pioneering themes touching the church.[42]

---

systematization we find successive forms employing intellectual resources bound to complex historical interplays' ('Herméneutique de saint Thomas', in *Revue des sciences philosophiques et théologiques* 57 [1973]: 611).

39. *Fifty Years of Catholic Theology: Conversations with Yves Congar,* 52. For Congar's remarks on authority and freedom in the church born of the controversy over priest workers see Yves Congar, 'Autorité et liberté dans l'Église', in *À Temps et à contretemps: Retrouver dans l'Église le visage de Jésus-Christ* (Paris: Cerf, 1969).
40. Congar, 'L'Avenir de l'Église', in *Écrits réformateurs,* 367–69.
41. Jossua, 'Yves Congar: La vie et l'Oeuvre d'un Théologien', 1.
42. Joseph Famerée, 'Originalité de l'écclésiologie du Père Congar', in *Bulletin de littérature*

There are still struggles within the church over whether a timeless Baroque ontology or the salvation history of the Spirit is to guide. 'Congar developed his own, original position, one between the impenitent optimism of his old friend Chenu, and the increasing pessimism of Bouyer, Daniélou, Hâmer, Journet, and de Lubac.'[43] Amid the developments and controversies after the council, Congar remained calm, pointing out the value of the great themes of the council and urging freedom of research.

To read Congar today is to be struck by his passion for the future. He wrote many pages, many essays about *'l'avenir'*. His courage during years of persecution was empowered by a study of history and was borne forward by a hopeful understanding of the church's potential for healthy self-realization. Yves Congar's theology of church and tradition and ministry is not about the end of anything or about a restoration or reform of what was antiquated and shallow, dynamics that Congar detected in the policies of John Paul II. The on-going life of the church flows normally from the primal dynamic of the Spirit and from educated and active men and women empowered by community.[44]

Pope John Paul II honored Congar a year before his death by making him a cardinal in recognition of his life's work as a theologian. Close friends of his saw that Congar was pleased to be made a cardinal by the same Holy See that had been for so many years cruel to him and hostile to his thought. It was a sort of vindication of his many sacrifices.

How remarkable it is that someone living a vowed religious life, working as a theologian constrained by the late-Baroque papacy, and persecuted as a pioneer of renewal was summed up at the time of his death by the Paris newspapers as 'a free man.'[45]

---

ecclésiastique 106 (2005): 111.

43. Fouilloux, 'Un théologien dans l'Église du XXe Siècle', 38.

44. See the essays in René Rémond, editor, *Le Concile de Vatican II: Son Église—Peuple de Dieu et corps du Christ* (Paris: Beauchesne, 1984). 'For me what has been most profound is to take on the stance of John the Baptist. I am not the Bridegroom [the Christ]. And you must be content with what you are. I am the antechamber, the door. Each has his vocation, and for each person that vocation is the most beautiful. I don't compare myself, absolutely not, to anyone else—that is idiotic—and I don't want others to compare themselves to me. To each person belongs what is most his, most hers—that is what is most beautiful (cited in 'Yves Congar: La vie et l'oeuvre d'un théologien', in *Cristianesimo nella Storia* 17 [1996]: 11). 'It would be a betrayal of *aggiornamento* to think that it was fixed once and for all in the texts of Vatican II', 9)

45. Jean-Pierre Manigne, 'Le Père Congar, Un Homme Libre', in *La Vie* (10 November 1994): 11.

Chapter 4

Louis-Joseph Lebret: Economist and Prophet

When *Gaudium et Spes* (The Pastoral Constitution on the Church in the Modern World) was published in December of 1965, readers were struck by the tone of its long introduction (§4-10). It spoke about the aspirations of people worldwide and about responding to the 'real social and cultural transformation' of the world. It addressed the options facing society in stark terms: a world of abundance in which so many people are plagued by hunger, where people yearning for freedom are confronted with new forms of social and psychological slavery. New ideas had called many traditional values into question. All these challenges posed fundamental questions: What is humanity? What is the purpose of human progress? This was an unprecedented perspective—that 'the council, relying on the inspiration of Christ . . . proposes to speak to all people in order to unfold the mystery that is humankind and to cooperate in tackling the main problems facing the world today' (§10). Never before had an ecumenical council addressed itself to the whole of humanity like this.

French Dominican economist Louis-Joseph Lebret had played a key role in shaping these lines. Lebret was known in Europe as a thinker who saw the gospel as a message not just for Christians, but for all humanity. Along with the secretary of the subcommission on 'the signs of the times', Lebret composed a draft for the constitution's introduction.[1] In his view, social justice was not about abstract moral obligations, but about the collective aspirations of humanity. As the constitution's §9 puts it: 'Women and men as individuals and as members of society crave a life that is

---

1. Philippe Bordeyne, 'L'Appel à la justice face au désir d'être plus homme: L'Apport de Louis-Joseph Lebret à la rédaction de *Gaudium et Spes*' (Paper read at the conference, *The Call to Justice: The Legacy of Gaudium et Spes 40 Years Later*, Vatican City, March 16–18, 2005), 3.

full, autonomous, and worthy of their nature as human beings; they long to harness for their own welfare the immense resources of the modern world.' Lebret aimed to put the church in dialogue with the world in a way that would touch every human heart.

Setting Sail

The name Lebret is related to the words *le Breton* (someone from Brittany). That is apt. Louis-Joseph Lebret was born in 1897 at Minihic-sur-Rance, a small village near Saint-Malo on the north coast of Brittany. The son of a naval carpenter, Lebret grew up surrounded by the sea. At seventeen, he entered the Brest Naval Academy from which he graduated as a naval officer. He spent the First World War aboard a torpedo chaser. By 1921 he had become the traffic manager of the Port of Beirut in Lebanon, which was governed by France at that time. He was awarded the Legion of Honor in 1923.

This looked like the beginning of a distinguished naval career. Secretly, however, Louis Lebret had long considered a religious vocation. He sampled Trappist life at the monastery of Briquebec near his home, but after a brief stay recognised that he was a man of action who could not do without some apostolic expression. However, he made a fundamental decision there. He decided to give his life to God.

At the age of twenty-six, Lebret entered the Dominican novitiate of the province of Lyons at Angers. He chose to become a friar preacher. Years later Lebret wrote for people considering apostolic involvement in the church:

> Set out! You can't know what ships you'll meet, what storms will soak you to the skin, or in what harbors you will weigh anchor. You take off without foreseeing all that lies ahead, and you will arrive somewhere. There is certainly risk; but don't let that keep you from setting off on your voyage.[2]

By all odds he was taking a risk in leaving behind what many would have considered a path to fame and glory.

---

2. François Malley, *Le Père Lebret: L'Economie au service des hommes* (Paris: Editions du Cerf, 1968), 9.

After his novitiate in France, Lebret was sent to Rijckholt, Holland, where his province's study program was because of the government's expulsion of Catholic seminaries. He had the good fortune to find mentors who inspired him. One of these was Sertillanges, who had been banished to Holland after his famous sermon at the Church of the Madeleine in Paris expressing dissent from the pope's political advice about France's relations with Germany.

Sertillanges modeled the man of action that Lebret aspired to be, showing him what courage and intelligence can do. Sertillanges was what we call today a 'public intellectual', someone who took people's social and spiritual well-being seriously and found ways to articulate their hopes and move their hearts. In Rijckholt Lebret probably never dreamed that he would fill that same role with distinction someday.

Lebret studied hard and became solidly grounded in St Thomas Aquinas' theology. However, the study program had a negative effect on his health. Following his ordination in 1929, he fell ill, humorously describing his ailment as 'severe metaphysicsitis', a withering reaction to too much abstract thinking. He was extremely tired, and his superiors sent him for a period of rest in Brittany in the priory of Paramé near Saint-Malo. He joined a small community of Dominicans who were loved by the people of the region. He took long walks along the coast and soon discovered his life's mission.

The Mission to Fishermen

At the end of the First World War in 1918, the French economy was depressed. In northwestern France, big fishing companies were forcing small, family fishing operations out of business. With unlimited financial resources, the big companies (many international) had developed methods of seizing huge quantities of fish, emptying the fishing fields of the region, and marketing the fish in massive quantities. Faced with this competition, local small fishermen barely had the money to keep their boats and equipment afloat, much less money to acquire new vessels and equipment. Consequently the whole character of an industry for people who had made their livelihood at sea for centuries was disrupted.

Visiting the neighboring areas, Lebret saw the results and reflected on their consequences. He spent hours and days talking to the fishermen, to their wives and families, and to fish merchants as well. Visiting them in their homes, he saw their poverty, their loss of dignity, and their feelings of helplessness. Their poverty was not just economic, but social and spiritual as well. Gradually he visited all the ports along the coast and tried to study the causes of their distress and ways to counteract it.

One of these fishermen, Ernest Lamort, became his first great right-hand man. After Lebret's first visit to their home, Madame Lamort warned her husband, 'Be careful of this monk—he's going to get you involved.'[3] Lebret recognised talent and drew valuable people into his projects. With Lamort, Lebret identified and analysed the situation. He saw that the suffering of the maritime world of Brittany was not just about the local economy, but also about the violent disregard for people and human consequences that characterises capitalism. Here began Lebret's lifelong commitment to social analysis and the promotion of human development. As he came up with concrete solutions for the problems at hand, he also began studying economics and sociology.

In order to marshal economic assistance for families suffering from the crisis of the fishing industry, Lebret and Lamort founded the Maritime Social Secretariat. Most of the 40,000 fishermen in Brittany were forced to sell their catch at a loss. Many of them had only occasional employment or none at all. The Secretariat, in cooperation with the French national federation of maritime trade unions, the French national school of social work (*L'École Normale Sociale*), and other interested organizations, worked to bring about new standards that would affect not only the fishermen, but also wholesalers, transport companies, and the factories that canned the fish. In a March, 1933 article, Lebret described his goals this way:

> We are acting under the banner of corporate responsibility.
> We need to relieve the state government of its excessive concerns, leaving to it the role of making only genuinely indispensible interventions. We need to empower the various parts of the profession to work together in writing the laws . . . [W]e need to rebuild the profession and let it take care of itself.[4]

Some years later, Lebret would articulate the convictions that guided him during these initial undertakings at Saint-Malo. They became basic principles that developed as the scope of his influence grew. To paraphrase them:

---

3. Malley, *Le Père Lebret: L'Economie au service des hommes*, 30.
4. *La Voix du Marin*, 9 (March, 1933), cited in Malley, *Le Père Lebret: L'Economie au service des hommes*, 37.

1. Feel mercy in your gut: get people out of dehumanizing situations. Form community with them and embrace their destiny. Close contact with human misery opens your eyes.

2. Analyse all the facts of the situation: get in touch with the objects of your concern through direct observation and meticulous detail. In order to clarify for yourself what's going on and to convince others, use photos, films—create a visual, living synthesis of what you see.

3. Think out your initiatives carefully. Take counsel, discuss. (One of the keys to the success of the Maritime Social Secretariat was its regular research seminars with invited experts who came to share and reflect on the situation.)

4. Educate people. Lebret was in favor of directly confronting burning issues; he had an infectious way of describing the need for action and for change. He freely delegated responsibility to others who became disciples in his cause.

5. Collaborate with the laity. This was not just a tactic, but a fundamental principle. This is what society and church should be like: people should be responsible for their own destiny. He had a talent for guiding ordinary people into leadership. (Lebret along with Canon Havard of Saint-Malo founded the *Jeunesse Maritime Chrétienne* [Young Christian Seamen] to provide an intellectual and spiritual formation to young adults in the region and help them adopt an apostolic attitude toward their profession.)

6. Take responsibility for some segment of society and plunge yourself into it, don't look on from outside. What people in trouble need is not paternalism, but development. In this regard, Lebret always remained wary of the danger of administrative approaches that operated from above, instead of from inside. He understood that 'it is a grace when the group takes you in as one of their own'.

7. Human development is linked to evangelization. Although development can't dispense with concrete methods, the vision and the goal must come from faith. In Lebret's words: 'The goal of an organization for development is not to Christianise the milieu, but rather to make it fully human, thus creating conditions for living more easily as a Christian.'[5]

These principles are the fruit of his experience, expressing his response to the situation in France at the end of the Second World War and to the social changes that the war had introduced. Lebret was confident that people could transform their own lives for the better, given the chance. But they needed leadership.

Theology and Ministry in a Transformed Society

To understand Lebret's ideas, it is crucial to know the context that inspired them. The impact of the Nazi occupation that began in 1940 cannot be overestimated. As Jean-Marie Domenach and Robert de Montvalon observed, the defeat of the French was more than a political defeat. It was a clear sign of the need for a new social order. This military and political debacle inspired seeds of hope for a different kind of nation in many French intellectuals. They set out to imagine a better world.

The principal example, already mentioned, is the book published in 1943 by two French priests, Henri Godin and Yvan Daniel, *La France, Pays de Mission?* (*Is France a Mission Land?*). It stirred strong reactions across the country. It frankly described the dechristianization of the working classes and the bourgeois culture of Catholic parishes. The authors emphasised that the church's primary goal is not to improve the personal morals of individuals, but to build life-giving communities of faith and charity. The preoccupation of bourgeois Catholics was what was *respectable*: good taste trumping the common good. This led to compulsive moral individualism that had nothing to offer to the poor and the unemployed, the undereducated and the disenchanted. As a result, French people didn't hear the Gospel preached to them, because the preaching of the time was completely absorbed with churchy questions that had nothing to do with the interests and struggles of real life.[6]

---

5. L-J Lebret, *De l'efficacité politique du chrétien* (Paris: Economie et Humanisme, 1946), 101–102; cited in Malley, *Le Père Lebret: L'Economie au service des hommes,* 28–34.
6. Jean-Marie Domenach and Robert de Montvalon, *The Catholic Avant-Garde: French*

The archbishop of Paris, Cardinal Suhard, supported the approach of Godin and Daniel, and he wrote in parallel fashion: 'We have to reach out to souls in order to save them, and become fearlessly involved, when necessary, in the [secular] and social spheres, because the divine will and the law of the Gospel are there too. That is the road whereby many souls can be reached and saved.'[7]

This explains Lebret's passionate concern with social and economic questions. The French had been exposed principally to three social doctrines, Capitalism, Marxism, and National Socialism. Christian doctrine was absent from this dialog precisely because it showed no interest in economic and social problems. Lebret put it this way: 'Three dynamic ideas excite people today: the mirage of communism, the prestige of nationalism [Nazism], and the right to make profit off of money [capitalism]. What can we do when swamped by these waves of greed and human desire?"[8]

Lebret was convinced that an authentic account of Christian doctrine is more humane, realistic, and helpful than any of these competing ideologies. But pastors and theologians have to be interested in questions related to political action and social destiny. With the help of the economist René Moreux, another collaborator at Saint-Malo, Lebret undertook a systematic study of Marxism as a starting point for addressing the combined challenge of unrestrained profit capitalism and the progressive degradation of the human condition caused by industrialised mass poverty.

These words of the Russian philosopher Nicolas Berdyaev (living in France at the time) might have come from Lebret's pen: 'The divorce of the economy from life, the technical interpretation of life, and the fundamental capitalist principle of profit, transform man's economic life into a fiction.'[9] In other words, the participation of ordinary citizens in their political and economic destiny was merely an illusion, when in reality jobs, markets, social ideas, and the prevailing vision of a healthy economy were controlled by a small oligarchy composed of captains of industry and the politicians profiting from their support.

Lebret was convinced that the disorder in both France and the world economy was a much larger question than the problems of the fishing

Catholicism since World War II (New York: Holt, Rinehart and Winston, 1967), 48–53.
7. Jean-Marie Domenach and Robert de Montvalon, *The Catholic Avant-Garde*, 53.
8. Lebret, 'Mystique de la conquête', cited in Malley, *Le Père Lebret: L'Economie au service des hommes*, 53.
9. Nicolas Berdyaev, *The Meaning of History*, translated by George Reavey (London, Centenary Press, 1936), 219.

industry. In September, 1941, he founded a new organization to study and analyse economic and social conditions scientifically, developing a social teaching that would put the economy at the service of humanity and forming professional collaborators who would be able to put the common good at the center of an association for reorganising the economy. Lebret's dream was to develop study centers, workshops, periodicals, conferences, and a network of professional collaborators who understood and believed in the common good.

This new organisation, called *Economy and Humanism*, began its existence with a small office in Marseilles. One of its first publications, a manifesto declaring the vision of the group, included these points: the rejection of a profit economy, a structural reform of social institutions, a clear distinction between desired goods and real human necessities, and the articulation of a communitarian economy. This constituted a formidable challenge. In Lebret's words:

> Our contemporary world is not like a house that needs to be rebuilt, but like a sick organism that needs to be healed. You can rebuild a house from outside, but you can only heal a sick organism from within . . . All things considered, technology should adapt to human needs and to the common good, not humanity to unbridled technology. The norm must be the moral and physical health of persons.[10]

Being actually involved with the society in need of development was fundamental to Lebret's program, and this attracted one of his most important Dominican colleagues to Economy and Humanism. In 1944, Jacques Loew, a recently ordained Dominican, came to Marseilles to join his team. Following Lebret's advice, Loew began to study the dockers at the Port of Marseilles, using a methodology that today we would describe as 'participant observation'. Loew became a docker himself and befriended this hard-working, rough crowd of laborers whose activities were so vital to the port. He thus became one of the first worker-priests. Even though Loew's participation in Economy and Humanism was brief, his on-site study became a model for such studies that the association would undertake in the future, and he and Lebret remained in contact in the coming years.

---

10. *Manifeste d'Économie et Humanisme*, 59–60.

In 1942, Economy and Humanism began publishing a technical journal of the same name to disseminate the team's research. During the war years this was difficult, since paper was scarce and long-distance communication far from easy. But the publication filled a void since very little was being done to study the French economy critically. During the 1940s, the group also began convening research seminars and workshops composed of theologians, Dominican colleagues, university professors from Toulouse and Aix-en-Provence, industrialists, and representatives of Catholic Action movements. These sessions would become a fixture of Economy and Humanism for decades. Lasting a weekend or sometimes up to a week, they were a forum for presenting new research and getting feedback from academic and professional peers, and they initiated a good number of participants into the basic ideas of the movement. These sessions not only provided many pastors and Catholic teachers with their social formation, but also gave influential government and business leaders a new way of looking at economic questions.

Re-Centering on Lyons: Christ is the Common Good of Humanity

Lebret never thought of Marseilles as the ideal site for his project, since he wanted to reach out to the entire nation and Marseilles was far from the center of France. In the summer of 1943, the Dominican Provincial of Lyons informed Lebret that the province had purchased a large property close to the town of L'Arbresle (about twenty miles northeast of Lyons) where they hoped to construct a new research center and house of studies. As the Provincial put it, 'This could become a great Dominican center, a large priory filled with liturgical song, right near the city of Lyons', where there could be a retreat house and a school for social education and religious studies that would attract many, especially young people.[11]

Lebret was enchanted, even though it would be another fifteen years before the Priory of La Tourette, Le Corbusier's architectural gem, would be erected there. The property had an old chateau and some farm buildings, and Lebret relocated his foundation there for the next several years. The landscape was stunning, at the southern tip of the Beaujolais wine region. Rolling hills and vast horizons with the mountains of the Massif Central visible in the distance provided a refreshing landscape, and the train station of L'Arbresle was a fifteen minute stroll away. Hundreds made that short trip from Lyons to Economy and Humanism.

---

11. Malley, *Le Père Lebret: L'Economie au service des hommes*, 68.

Lebret kept exploring the fundamental idea at the base of his social thinking, the common good. He always thought of humanity as a universal family with one divine origin and one common destiny. The common good, he thought, has to be the foundation for social justice and right government. His notion of the common good, therefore, was not rooted either in intuition or in rational principles, but rather in experience. It is 'the totality of social conditions that allows groups and their members to achieve their full flourishing more easily and completely'.[12]

The common good is more than the sum of what is good for individuals. It is more than assuring each person the right to do what he or she wishes. 'It is a good which is created through the collaborative effort of all people, and it flows back to enrich them all without being segmented into separate concerns. It is the good that creates and strengthens a human community. It pertains, then, to all levels of human experience: families, businesses, professions, local collectivities, and nations.'[13] For Lebret, this was not theoretical idealism, but a pragmatic expression of his own experiences of helping people to cooperate with one another.

In addition, the common good was not just about material factors, but spiritual as well. 'The spiritual common good', he wrote

> is the total potential of intelligence, scientific understanding,
> wisdom, and social skills; of intellectual, moral, artistic and
> pedagogical traditions; the potential of humanity's material
> masterpieces and its institutions as well. It is culture, human-
> ism—all of it leading to an eternal destiny. God is in fact the
> absolute and transcendent common good for human beings,
> just as God is their origin and their fulfillment. Christ is the
> common good of humanity . . . [14]

Although this theological affirmation did not ordinarily find expression in Lebret's technical and scientific works, it remained the inspiration and the foundation for his social thinking. Lebret thought that misunderstanding the nature of the common good was the principal reason that the western nations had fallen into economic and moral decay and into their deadly

---

12. Paul Houée, *Un éveilleur d'humanité: Louis-Joseph Lebret* (Paris: Editions de l'Atelier, 1997) 20.
13. Paul Houée, *Un éveilleur d'humanité*, 20.
14. Paul Houée, *Un éveilleur d'humanité*, 21.

confrontations over economic interests and power. In the context of the Cold War, Lebret dared to articulate a concern for all of humanity based on the principle of the common good.

His idea of the common good 'embraces everything human, every single person, and works under all kinds of social conditions'.[15] Although Lebret was not proposing a political system, he realised that there had to be some recognised authority to guarantee a common good that would be accepted by representative assemblies and be in dialogue with regional and professional interests. This became his key inspiration, and he never stopped trying to articulate it in ways that might lead to international co-operation.

If Lebret's ideas seem naïve or unrealistic today, we should remember that he was a notable interpreter of the social teaching of the twentieth century popes. Pope Pius XI, in his encyclical *Quadragesimo anno*, published in 1931, spoke in similar phrases:

> The distribution of created goods, which, as every discerning person knows, is laboring today under the gravest evils due to the huge disparity between the few exceedingly rich and the unnumbered propertyless, must be effectively called back to and brought into conformity with the norms of the common good, that is, social justice.[16]

In 1942, in the first issue of the review *Économie et Humanisme*, Lebret explained that in a rational hierarchy of goods, human needs and spiritual goods must take primacy over profit. Respect for nature and for biological rhythms supersedes mechanical and industrial rhythms in dignity and importance. Then he went on to say:

> Economic chaos begins when the masters of the economy think of workers as resources, not persons; when they exploit labor to magnify profits. Thus to claim the riches of the planet for several thousand privileged rich people, to organize production and markets uniquely for their benefit; to close borders to workers when countries have great resources is

15. Paul Houée, *Un éveilleur d'humanité*, 21.
16. *Acta Apostolicae Sedis* (1931), 197; cited in *Compendium of the Social Doctrine of the Church* (Libreria Editrice Vaticana, 2004), 95.

unjust. People have a right to share in a reasonable way the work and the fruits of the land.[17]

Development is the New Name for Peace

In 1945, Père Lebret began traveling to gather research data and to disseminate his ideas. He visited Belgium, Luxembourg, Germany, Switzerland, Denmark and Sweden to study their social organization and analyse their economies. In 1947, he was invited to teach a course about the principles of Economy and Humanism at the School of Social Sciences in São Paulo, Brazil. He was received enthusiastically. For the first time he saw the disgraceful poverty and oppression of the shantytown slums of Latin America. He also met Dom Helder Camara, the Bishop of Recife, who became a life-long supporter and who would depend upon Lebret for technical help at Vatican II.

Thus began years of consultation, teaching, and research in many nations, especially in Latin America. He travelled and lectured in Uruguay, Argentina, Chile, and Colombia; then later in Vietnam, Dahomey (today Benin), and Senegal (where he became personal advisor about economic affairs and development to the president). Lebret earned an international reputation from these travels that included consultations with top national leaders. These experiences led Lebret to conclude that 'development is the problem of the century'.[18] But he failed to persuade his colleagues at Economy and Humanism to make international development their principal focus. So he set out once again as a founder to inaugurate IRFED, the *Institut International de Recherche et de Formation en vue du Développement Harmonisé* (Institute for Research and Training for Harmonized Development) also located in Lyons.

IRFED also created study programs and seminars of short duration, bringing students to France from Latin America, Africa and the Middle East. IRFED 'would have a major influence in the formation of Latin American leaders during the 1960s'.[19] Lebret saw the need for a new publication which became IRFED's journal *Développement et Civilisation*. In it he published the results of his studies on Latin America, Vietnam, Leba-

---

17. *Economie et Humanisme*, 6 (1944): 240–241.
18. Malley, *Le Père Lebret: L'Economie au service des hommes*, 94.
19. Jean-Claude Lavigne and Hugues Puel, 'For a Human-Centered Economy: Louis-Joseph Lebret (1897–1966)' in Francesco Compagnoni and Helen Alford, editors, *Preaching Justice: Dominican Contributions to Social Ethics in the Twentieth Century* (Dublin: Dominican Publications, 2007), 103.

non and Africa, as well as research reports from the IRFED team. As a result, Lebret's name was becoming better known at the United Nations and in European universities. He was widely considered a clear-sighted thinker in the area of planning and development for the world economy and was often invited to participate in international meetings.

Influencing the Local Church

In France in the 1940s and 50s religious sociology played a pastoral role. Dioceses and religious congregations began to depend upon pastoral planning to shape their response to the needs of the people they served. Lebret and his team at Economy and Humanism became involved in this kind of analysis and respected for their comprehensive approach. French bishops invited Lebret to develop sociological studies of French pastoral life and to offer workshop to priests and seminarians on his findings. He integrated the church's social teaching into his analysis of pastoral life.

Encouraged by some French bishops early in the 1950s, Lebret met the papal nuncio in Paris, Archbishop Roncalli, and through him became acquainted with Archbishop Montini at the Secretariat of State in the Vatican. This led to his important and lasting relationship with the future Pope Paul VI. Following Roncalli's election as Pope John XXIII in 1958, Lebret stayed in touch with his Vatican contacts. John XXIII received him in a private audience in spring of 1960. Lebret was encouraged by Pope John's encyclicals *Mater et Magistra* (1961) and *Pacem in Terris* (1962) because of their concern for underdeveloped countries and for solidarity with the entire world. However, Lebret felt that their analysis and recommendations were insufficient. He was wary of documents that could be read as moral exhortations rather than as structural analysis of real social and economic conditions. He would soon have a chance to introduce his analysis of international social dysfunction into official statements of the church.

In 1962, during Vatican II's first session, Lebret was conducting research and lecturing in Madagascar, Egypt, Senegal and Lebanon. About that time, Lebret wrote these touching sentiments in his journal:

> You have to be young to do what I do. I have had to totally abandon Latin America. I have started working with Madagascar. I arrived in Senegal too late. I haven't given enough time to IRFED in Paris. As to deepening my work—almost nothing. Lebanon is eating me alive with a conflict where I

can learn a lot, but I don't have the energy to do what really needs to be done . . .

Now that everybody else has discovered development, how can we be effective with the international, multilateral, bilateral 'watchdogs', to say nothing of the private commercial businesses with colossal means that they so shamefully waste? It takes guts to go on, but I must. My voice, weak as it is, has to stand up for what humanity means. No doubt it is time to rethink our operations; they have become too scattered . . . I want to get back to reflection and writing. From now on, I should be more of a consultant than an operative . . . (Jan 1, 1963)[20]

As the first session of Vatican II came to an end, Cardinal Suenens of Belgium, with Cardinal Montini's support and Pope John's encouragement, proposed to the council the idea of a new document concerning the church's presence to the modern world. This proposal was accepted by the council fathers. Then Pope John XXIII died and was succeeded by Cardinal Montini as Pope Paul VI.

The new pope invited Lebret to represent the Vatican at a U.N. conference on international development in Geneva in 1963. At that conference, Lebret said, 'All the world's resources have to be employed in a way that will benefit the whole of humanity. The world needs a new economic order that will lead to a community of equitable opportunities and of universal respect for all cultures.'[21] His message was received positively and warmly at the conference. Later that year, Paul VI invited Lebret to be an expert at the council to assist in developing the council's Schema XIII, which was to become the Pastoral Constitution on the Church in the Modern World.

Lebret worked on a subcommission for Schema XIII on 'the signs of the times'. Fr François Houtart was the secretary of the subcommission, and he and Lebret drafted and edited the pages that led to the introduction to *Gaudium et Spes* mentioned above. Lebret's voice and influence are clearest in the section of the document addressing questions of international community (numbers 83 to 90). As number 83 states:

---

20. Journal extracts cited in Malley, *Le Père Lebret: L'Economie au service des hommes*, 165–6.
21. Paul Houée, *Un éveilleur d'humanité*, 179.

> If peace is to be established, the first condition is to root out those causes of discord between people which lead to wars, especially injustice. Much discord is caused by excessive economic inequalities and by delays in correcting them. Other causes are a desire for power and contempt for people, and at a deeper level, envy, distrust, pride and other selfish passions. People cannot put up with such an amount of disorder . . .

Gaudium et Spes' achievement, despite the struggle to produce it and the opposition of the conservative minority, was to articulate the church's real openness to universal human concerns, offer a sign of the church's solidarity with all who struggle for justice, and clearly affirm Lebret's favorite theme, that in becoming more human, people become more open and ready to receive the divine gifts of evangelization and grace.

Even while working on Schema XIII, Lebret was called upon for additional service to the Holy See. Exploring the possibility of a permanent Vatican secretariat on poverty, Paul VI asked Lebret to draft a document that became 'Elements for a Strategy of Christian Presence in the Task of Development'. In February 1965, Lebret drafted a paper analysing population and birth control, and he was appointed by the pope to the papal commission for the study of birth control.[22]

Occasionally Lebret was invited to private audiences with Paul VI who sought his advice on social problems. During one of these meetings, the pope shared his intention to write an encyclical on development, and he asked Lebret to draft what would become *Populorum Progressio*. In the summer of 1964, while on vacation in Brittany, Lebret wrote his first draft. In February, 1965, after further consultation with Paul VI he revised it. The pope was not sure whether to publish the encyclical before or after the end of the council. He did not want to unduly influence the council fathers, preferring to see how they would resolve their discussions on Schema XIII. So Lebret planted the seed for this papal teaching without knowing what the precise outcome would be. *Populorum Progressio* was published only at Easter 1967, a year after Lebret's death.

---

22. See Paul Houée, *Un éveilleur d'humanité*, 179; also Lavigne and Puel, 'For a Human-Centered Economy', 103f. Lavigne and Puel give an authoritative profile of the economic thought and social theology of Lebret that is considerably more detailed than what is presented here.

Paul VI pays tribute to Lebret in paragraph 14 of the encyclical, saying: 'As an eminent specialist on this question [citing Lebret in a footnote] has rightly said: "We cannot allow economics to be separated from human realities, nor development from the civilization in which it takes place. What counts for us is the human person—each individual human person, each human group, and humanity as a whole."'[23] Many passages ring with the unmistakable themes that Lebret had elaborated over the years. Here is a sample:

> What are less than human conditions? The material poverty of those who lack the bare necessities of life, and the moral poverty of those who are crushed under the weight of their own self-love; oppressive political structures resulting from the abuse of ownership or the improper exercise of power, from the exploitation of the worker or unjust transactions. What are truly human conditions? The rise from poverty to the acquisition of life's necessities; the elimination of social ills; broadening their horizons of knowledge; acquiring refinement and culture. From there one can go on to acquire a growing awareness of other people's dignity, a taste for the spirit of poverty, an active interest in the common good, and a desire for peace.

The encyclical *Populorum Progressio* goes on to insist that economic programs should have only one aim—to serve humanity, reduce inequities, eliminate discrimination, free people from the burdens of servitude (n. 34). Economic development must mean social progress as well as economic growth. Then, paragraph 76 of the encyclical uses a phrase that has become legendary:

> *Development is the new name for peace* . . . For peace is not simply the absence of warfare, based on a precarious balance of power; it is fashioned by efforts directed day after day toward the establishment of the ordered universe willed by God, with a more perfect form of justice among all people.

---

23. The text of the encyclical is available online at www.vatican.va/holy_father/paul_vi/ encyclicals/

In the spirit of the council the encyclical elaborates themes in *Gaudium et Spes* concerning international cooperation and development. In addition to being a tribute from the Holy See to Lebret's lifelong work, the encyclical is an authoritative dissemination of his key ideas and principles in the church's social teaching. In 1967, Pope Paul VI established the Pontifical Commission for Justice and Peace as an organism of the universal church to promote the justice and love of Christ toward the poor and to promote international social justice. In this same spirit, in 1968, the pope designated New Year's Day as the World Day of Peace.

In Service to the Third World Bishops at the Council

During the third session of the council (September to November, 1964), Lebret's consultations with the French bishops were more intense. His role among the bishops of Latin America and Vietnam was even more important. He helped the bishops of the Third World formulate interventions at the council and helped them to 'de-westernise' the council's discussions. Mostly these activities occurred at meetings and dinners rather than in the commissions. When Dom Helder Camara took the floor at the council assembly, he often enunciated insights that arose from Lebret's sessions with the Latin American bishops.

For the subcommission, Lebret had to review and analyse some 20,000 interventions concerning the drafting of Schema XIII. During the intersession of February 1964, he joined a working group of bishops, experts, and lay advisors at a meeting held in the Italian countryside at Arrica to work on reshaping the document. Concerning that meeting, he wrote: 'What a joy to encounter a church fully alive with a sense of communion with the whole of humanity.'[24] Meanwhile, Lebret continued traveling to consult with world leaders under the banner of IRFED, for research in Africa and Lebanon, and doing some teaching (especially a course in Rome for those studying at the Pontifical Ecclesiastical Academy, the training center for future nuncios).

In April, 1965, Père Lebret was hospitalised for several ailments and for chronic fatigue. His illness proved to be cancer. He underwent multiple surgeries and then chemotherapy. During his convalescence he continued to review and revise texts for Schema XIII and for other Vatican projects. During the fourth session of the council, Schema XIII, now the Pastoral

---

24. Houée, *Un éveilleur d'humanité*, 179.

Constitution on the Church in the Modern World, was finished and adopted by a vote of 2111 in favor and 251 against. A subsequent vote for ratification on December 7 was even stronger, with 2309 in favor and only 75 against. Pope Paul VI's promulgation of this pastoral constitution with the title *Gaudium et Spes* on December 8, 1965, was one of the last acts of Vatican II.

What Did His Life Mean?

The dreams of the boy became the achievements of the man. The boy Louis Lebret, breathing sea air scented with the kelp and iodine of the Brittany coast, watching boats enter and leave the great harbor of Saint-Malo, dreamed of the day that he too might someday visit foreign shores in Africa, America, and the Middle East. He could never have imagined how his vision would be fulfilled. He would not only visit foreign shores, but bring to those lands a vision of justice and humanity that had been planted in him from his earliest days among Breton fishermen. His years as a naval officer deepened the mystery of the sea and the allure of exotic destinations. But he needed more than that, and he dared to enter Dominican community life where other gifted idealists would help him refine his conviction that he too was meant to be an evangeliser and, why not, a prophet.

He discovered his missionary vocation in visiting his Breton neighbors and listening to their needs. In all his undertakings, Economy and Humanism, IRFED, his consultations with Third World national governments, and his assistance to the Holy See, Lebret's eyes were fixed on human needs and possibilities. His native environment and his early Christian education convinced him that every person deserves respect and that everyone has to look out for everyone else. His mantra about the ascent of the human to its full potential articulated an understanding of the common good that was not abstract, but based on his experience that people can always cooperate, despite class, ideology, or power. For him, the common good meant the ways that people found to cooperate as peers.

Lebret has been criticised as idealistic or naïve because he insisted that people are more important than profit, that community is more important than individual freedom, and that cooperation is more important than competition. However, he succeeded in unmasking the naïveté of those who called him naïve. He exposed their worship of the profit motive as the bogus 'spirituality' of capitalism, their claims for equal opportunity (available only to the powerful and rich) as cryptic greed, and their mystical confidence in the 'invisible hand' of capitalism as a force that invariably makes the rich richer and the poor poorer. His instincts led him to the heart of difficult social questions, studying them and discussing them with the smartest people he could find, and then formulating a new approach that levels the playing field so that all can participate. He dazzled people, both in the academic world and in politics, by his courage and his clarity. This down to earth prophet touched the hearts not only of politicians and the poor, but of economists and popes as well.

In his last years, Lebret recorded some observations in his journal that are in retrospect very touching:

> What can our little private centers, attempting to be independent, achieve in the face of monstrous inescapable new forces? Here is where the Gospel shows its stuff. The obstinate love in the hearts of people who want to be connected with everything in society, from top to bottom, is the love of those who are involved and active and responsive. This is what God wants from us; and here our redemptive and constructive efforts have a chance, even though they will face many apparent contradictions. The Council has given me the impression of a church in full rebirth that has become aware in a more critical way of its tasks to be *Mater et Magistra* (Mother and Teacher) at just the right moment, and to extend a welcome to everyone and to open itself to new and unprecedented tasks. (December 30, 1963)

And then shortly before his death, he wrote:

> Here I am in my room in Caluire [a suburb of Lyons]. What a shame that I am so rarely here . . . With respect to my illness, if the crisis in the area of my body burned by the chemo stops, I think that I will be able to lead a useful life, but one a lot less active and much different. Still, I'm hoping by September to start writing some books I've put off for a long time. I can't wait (July, 1966).

On the 20th July 1966, only days after that last entry, Lebret went to the Lord. He had indeed been drenched by storms, had weighed anchor in many ports, known both doldrums and tempests on his long voyage. But he had not allowed risks to hold him back and had sailed on in spite of them. And at last he came into port; not, however, before leaving behind him a log of his many journeys that continues to challenge and encourage those who pay attention to his story.

Chapter 5

Jacques Loew: Ministry on the Docks

In 1941, a Dominican priest Jacques Loew began an unusual, almost revolutionary form of ministry: he got a job working on the docks at the port of Marseilles, France. He could little imagine the reverberations in the church and in society of a Catholic priest finding a job, earning a wage, and living in a poor apartment house. For his goal was ministering to the people in the area, and he had discovered a new approach: serving and preaching the Gospel by working as well as living in a neighborhood. More than a hundred other French Catholics would follow him, combining work and priesthood. That movement would have effects on the economy of the French working class and on the self-understanding of the Roman Catholic Church. It contributed to a reappraisal of the priest's vocation and refashioned the relationship of the church to society. Praying and working, being a friar and a dock-worker, celebrating Mass for free but loading ships for money—that would bring Jacques Loew fame around the world and hostility in the corridors of the Vatican.

En route to the Dominicans and the Priesthood

Jacques Loew was born on the 31st August 1908, the only child in a family of non-believers in Clermont-Ferrand in southern France.[1] Baptised

---

1. Biographical studies include: R William Rauch [John Petrie], *The Worker-Priests. A Collective Documentation* (New York: Macmillan, 1956); Marie-Paule Préat, *Jacques Loew ou le défi évangélique* (Paris: Fayard-Mame, 1974); Jacques Loew, Dominique Xardel, *Le Bonheur d'être homme: Entretiens avec Dominique Xardel* (Paris: Centurion, 1988); François Leprieur, *Quand Rome condamne: Dominicains et prêtres-ouvriers* (Paris: Cerf, 1989); Jean Vinatier, *Les prêtres-ouvriers, le cardinal Liénart et Rome: Histoire d'une crise, 1944–1967* (Paris: Témoignage Chrétien, 1985); Bruno Duriez *et al*, editors, *Chrétiens et ouvriers en France 1937–1970* (Paris: Les Editions Ouvrières,

a Catholic, he was sent to a Protestant Sunday school and soon lost any interest in religion. His initial university studies were done in Nice, while his preparation for a career in law took place in Paris. He was a practicing lawyer in Nice until 1934 and later described himself as a convinced non-believer and no stranger to the casinos on the Riviera. While spending some months recovering from an illness in a sanatorium at Leysin in Switzerland, he read the New Testament and not long after at age twenty-four became in 1932 a practicing Catholic. At the suggestion of a friend, who was also on a journey to faith, he visited the Carthusian monastery of La Valsainte near Fribourg, Switzerland. In 1934, he entered the Dominicans and made his novitiate at Saint-Maximin, a magnificent medieval priory of the Toulouse Province of the Order of Preachers, located not far from Marseilles. He was ordained a priest in October, 1939.

An Early Priest-Worker

In 1941, he joined Father Louis-Joseph Lebret, a Dominican from a Breton family who had founded the movement *Économie et humanisme.* Lebret had worked from 1930 to 1939 among the fishermen of Saint-Malo whom he found to be defenseless against the ship owners and other exploiting groups. Drawing on a realistic sociology and a practical economics that were in their infancy, Lebret's center—in 1943 it moved from Marseilles to a town not far from Lyons—sought to let the grace of the Gospel illumine and improve social structures. That approach—religious and social—sought to explain and improve economic conditions by drawing on the values of justice in the Gospel.

Lebret sent Loew to study the conditions of the working classes in Marseille. Upon his arrival in 1941, Loew was frustrated by the lack of a helpful theory of change and by the distance between himself and people.

> Conduct statistical analyses? There have been scores of them, and they tell us precisely nothing. In the struggle to get be-

---

2001). Robert Masson, *Jacques Loew: Ce qui s'appelle la foi* (Saint-Maur: Parole et Silence, 2000) and Ulrich Engel, 'Bürgerliche Priester—Proletarische Priester. Ein Lehrstück aus der Konfliktgeschichte zwischen Kirche und Arbeiterschaft', *Gott der Menschen. Wegmarken dominikanischer Theologie* (Ostfildern: Matthias-Grünewald, 2010) offer a chronology and bibliographies. For bibliographical and archival material on Loew see Fondation Jacques Loew, rue des Chanoines 13, 1700 Fribourg, Switzerland with its website.

hind this poverty to the people themselves, there is, in fact,
only one way which so far the sociologists haven't tried: living it themselves. I concluded that it was no good wasting
time on paper theories. The thing to do was to buy overalls in
an old-clothes market, get a job like everyone else, and then
at the end of the day's work go off and live with the dregs of
the population—the dockers at the port.[2]

Would he not always be an outsider, a sociologist or a priest, unless he
shared their work? To live in the neighborhood or to serve in a nearby
church was not enough. Something more was needed—to work as they
did. He wanted to go beyond academic research and church buildings 'to
confront the socio-economic structures with a credible Christian humanism which begins with a precise knowledge of the obstacles in society, politics, and economics and then leads to a mission of evangelization.'[3] It was
not a question of identifying society or economics with faith but of seeing
their interpenetration. His audacious move into an apartment attracted
religious and priests, young and old church-goers, men and women. They
became pioneers in ministering to France's secularised industrial working
class.

Priests worked in plants assembling automobiles so that they could
share the life of those to whom they wanted to minister—now in a silent
or indirect way. Working alongside others in a factory was not a question
of image or symbolic presence; nor was life with the workers a form of
penance. At first, just being a priest made the poor suspicious of him; his
white Dominican habit was a sign of being an outsider, a strange man.

> I discover the extent to which the slum problem is bound
> up with the labor contract system; the congestion of certain
> families in miserable courtyards some hundreds of yards
> from the harbor is the inevitable condition of the miserable
> employment . . . I move in slowly. My nearest neighbor is

---

2. *Mission to the Poorest* (New York: Sheed and Ward, 1950), 22; (*En Mission prolétarienne* [Paris: L'Arbresle, 1946]).
3. François Leprieur, *Quand Rome condamne: Dominicains et prêtres-ouvriers,* 25; see 'Do
   the Baptised Have Rights? The French Worker-Priest Crisis of 1953–54', in John Orme
   Mills, *Justice, Peace, and Dominicans, 1216–2001* (Dublin: Dominican Publications,
   2001), 161–180.

a working-class prostitute, a poor woman who would like nothing better than to settle down in life. Opposite is the family with whom I shall live in the closest possible intimacy for two years: one room as lavatory for the whole house. The family consists of a grandfather, a grandmother, and a little girl of twelve."[4]

On January 1, 1942, he received his first paycheck.

A few months later three young women approached Loew about organising a pastoral team in Marseilles, and soon some priests and religious began a community for mission in the world of the dockworkers. The goal was not only to celebrate baptism and the Eucharist but to reduce poverty and suffering in any way possible. He soon founded the 'Mission de Marseille', and in 1943 the Bishop of Marseilles entrusted a working-class suburb to the priest-workers combining parish and mission. By 1944 (the Nazi occupation was going on during that experiment[5]) efforts had improved the Marseilles neighborhood, bringing a fixed wage and better working conditions. There were no books or classes for this apostolate: only, he said, contact with flesh-and-blood people. He wrote in 1944 a description of this new pastoral approach in *Les Dockers de Marseille – Analyse Type d'un Complexe*.[6] 'Some girls have not made their First Communion; they cannot read; they will be outcasts all their lives . . . What is to be done? It is quite simple—remove the lice and gently set the child back on the right track. That is where social service and the religious life dedicated to social service should begin.'[7] Loew served as a parish pastor while still working on the docks. In 1946 he published *En Mission prolétarienne*. He saw three basic directions for this approach: Christian life in community, pastoral engagement with the issues of the local area, and active participation in unions and other organisations.

---

4. *Mission to the Poorest*, 26, 37.
5. To minister to the large number of French sent by the Nazis to work in Germany, a number of priests, some openly, some secretly, accompanied them to work camps (Thomas Eggensperger, Ulrich Engel, *Dominikanerinnen und Dominikaner: Geschichte und Spiritualität* (Regensburg: Pustet, 2010) 111.
6. (Paris: Économie et humanisme, 1944 [second edition in 1946]).
7. *Mission to the Poorest*, 40.

How simple it is to live in a cell in a Dominican priory. There are no material needs, nothing to worry about. But I have learned that when you go out into the streets, when children throw their arms around you and men and women are happy to tell you about their lives, that is when I stop worrying. When you have a life that has no defenses against neighbors, each person comes to have, in their own way, a little place in your heart.[8]

Cardinal Emmanuel Suhard published in 1947 his pastoral letter on the problematical condition of the church in France: *Essor ou Déclin de l'Église* showed the need for new pastoral directions and anticipated some of the reforming motifs of Vatican II. Godin and Daniel's book, *La France, Pays de Mission?* from 1943, had analysed the proletarian milieu of Paris. Pointing out that some suburbs were de facto 'pagan', they dared to call France 'a missionary country'.[9] Laity and clergy joined Suhard in fashioning new organisations. The war brought to light the impotency of the old parish structure and also of the Catholic Action movement hesitantly sponsored by Rome. The Cardinal of Paris was furthering a new catechetics and liturgy. He supported priest-workers and even assigned priests to work in factories, hoping to draw the long alienated working class back to the parish churches.

Suhard founded his own 'Mission for France' in 1941 and set up a seminary for men whose zeal would embrace dynamic forms of priesthood. By the end of the war there were communities in Paris rooted in the working class areas where priests worked in factories. As Jacques Loew was developing his own mode of research and letting a pastoral theology emerge, the role of the laity and the mission of the baptised were increasingly discussed in France.[10] M-D Chenu composed theological position papers for urban ministries and concluded: 'The movement of the priest-workers is the most important religious movement since the French Revolution.'[11]

---

8. *Mission to the Poorest*, 74f.
9. Henri Godin, Yves David, *La France, Pays de Mission?* (Paris: Éditions de l'Abeille, 1943); on the rise of progressive movements in Paris, many allied to the Dominicans, see Yvon Tranvouez, *Catholiques et Communistes: La crise du progressisme Chrétien, 1950-1955* (Paris: Cerf, 2000).
10. Catherine Masson, 'Ruptures et renouveaux: la question des prêtres-ouvriers (1953–1965)', in *Mélanges de science religieuse* 61 (2004): 79.
11. Leprieur, *Quand Rome condamne*, 765. 'Is it not surprising to find Père Chenu at the

Loew found his Dominican education in the thought of Aquinas, drawing together nature and the grace, to help in overcoming the divisions placed everywhere by church and piety. Grace moved within people and communities. 'The supernatural is what is natural for God.'[12]

Paris and Marseilles witnessed a new kind of priest. The first priest-workers (*prêtres-ouvriers*) lived alone or, if they were religious, in groups of two or three; they were, however, catalysts in developing communities of religious and laity. Soon those groups active in labor and peace movements were at work in Lyons and Belgium, and by 1953 there were ninety priest-workers.[13] They could hardly avoid the strong presence of the Communist Party, and some joined Communist led unions rather than try to work with the less effective Catholic ones. A few of the priest-workers left the priesthood, and a few became dedicated Marxists.

While labor unions and other movements of solidarity and cooperation appeared to some pastors and bishops as alien groups, to the members of a religious order a team ministry had similarities with their community's way of life.[14] Dominican life suggested the structure of smaller self-directing communities within the parish and diocese. A contrast was clear between the church formed by the Baroque and continuing from 1850 to 1930 with its marked individual spirituality and attachment to religious objects, and the new quests after 1940 for community and worship according to biblical and patristic theologies. Loew emphasised the evangelizing mission of a new team approach but also the potential vitality of the parish church in new formats.

> Father Loew had developed at Marseilles an original pastoral style and an original mode of research. He was, however, reticent in terms of some further developments of the priests in the work place. The involvement of the parish was indispens-

founding session of the Mission de Paris at the end of 1943 among the priests of *Action populaire*? Even more, in terms of ideas Chenu became one of the most faithful and helpful companions of the *Mission de Paris* on its journey" (Leprieur, 24).

12. Loew cited in Robert Masson, *Jacques Loew: Ce qui s'appelle la foi*, 40.
13. Catherine Masson, 'Ruptures et renouveaux', 77. In 1951, Simone Weil who had met Loew wrote *La Condition ouvrière* (Paris: Gallimard, 1951).
14. For instance, an early priest-worker, coming from the Jocist movement, Henri Berger, OP, founded in 1949 the MRAP, a movement working against racism and anti-Semitism and for peace (Leprieur, *Quand Rome condamne*, 650–51).

able to him: manual work for priests was secondary (if necessary) and always needed to refer to parish ministry.[15]

Team ministry and activist social groups expanded incipient liturgical
participation and parish meetings. It was part of French Catholicism *en
marche*.[16]

The Vatican became alarmed at the priest-workers. There were reports
of them supporting economic and labor reforms. Were they not also involved in the volatile and widespread political ambitions of Socialism
and Communism in France? What shocked reactionary French Catholics
and Vatican bureaucrats about the priest-workers was a visible, symbolic
change. The priest was no longer defined by a black cassock, breviary, bi-
retta, and by living somewhat as a recluse in a rectory with a house-keeper.
That priest's lifestyle came from the nineteenth century and was part of the
inability of the hierarchical church (garbed in Baroque clothes) to address
men and women living in a modern culture with its secularity and freedom. Now, in ordinary clothes, a new kind of priest had appeared, a social
evangelist. Even if the priest-workers were a small percentage of diocesan
priests, their image was unnerving. Pius XII in 1953 called this new priest
'an object of scandal'.[17] Chenu advocated a theology and cultural history of
the priest that was not simply a reproduction of the socially marginalised
Baroque cleric. The constant reporting about priest-workers in the media
frightened affluent Catholics whose faith was private.

By 1945 Rome had already made its concerns known. The death of
Cardinal Suhard in 1949 and the departure in 1953 of Cardinal Roncalli
from being nuncio in Paris removed two strong defenders of the new pastoral efforts. In May, 1951, Loew had sent a long report defending the

---

15. Catherine Masson, 'Ruptures et renouveaux', 79. Yves Congar took part in 1953 at the
   second annual session of the *Mission de France* whose theme was the laity. He seemed
   to relativise the position of the priest-workers as he noted the dangers of that direction
   if the priesthood even in factories was dominant or exclusive. To make the apostolate
   or mission something for the priesthood alone, even in a new style, risked forgetting
   again lay people. He later said that his views were poorly received at those meetings
   (Masson, 'Ruptures et renouveaux', 79); see Jean Vinatier, *Le cardinal Suhard (1874–
   1949): l'évêque du renouveau missionnaire en France* (Paris: Le Centurion, 1983); *Le
   cardinal Liénart et la Mission de France* (Paris: Le Centurion, 1978).
16. Yvon Tranvouez, *Catholique d'Abord: Approches du movement catholique en France
   XIXe-XXe siècles* (Paris: Les Éditions Ouvrières, 1988).
17. Catherine Masson, 'Ruptures et renouveaux', 80.

movement's work to Giovanni Montini, the Vatican's assistant secretary of state and future Pope Paul VI. He met with Montini at that time in Rome and began a friendship with him. Pope Pius XII and his close advisers, however, were unrelenting and brought the experiment to a halt in 1954. 'This is a catastrophe for the church in France', exclaimed Cardinal Liénart.[18] In January, 1954, the bishops in France asked the priests to follow the command of the Vatican and by the 1st of March to leave their jobs in factories. Dozens of important figures in French public life protested, and almost half a million signatories registered their displeasure in letters.[19]

The priest-workers met at Villejuif, a suburb of Paris, in mid-February, 1954, to plan their reaction. The seven Jesuits among them had been withdrawn by their superiors. The eleven Dominicans responded in various ways; the vow of obedience and a clear fidelity to the Order made Loew an outsider, and he assured bishops and Dominican superiors that he would obey the rules of the Vatican and the decisions of his religious superiors. He continued to stress the ecclesial and spiritual aspect of the priest in the factory and to emphasise spirituality over the analysis of class struggle.

> What is the role of the priest-missionary in the present situation? How does he work to bring the souls of the workers to Christ, and how does he find a role in the workers' struggle? Where are these struggles leading? Would they help evangelize the proletariat? Going forward accentuates the differences. There is further the question of the orientation of the Christian laity, particularly of young people. Should only organizations with a strongly Marxist emphasis have an attraction for them?[20]

---

18. Catherine Masson, 'Ruptures et renouveaux', 81. Archbishop Richard J Cushing wrote in 1950 the 'Foreword' to a book by Loew: 'Catholics scandalized by social trends, fearful of what the future may bring, will be refreshed by the story of this Catholic sociologist of a most practical kind' ('Foreword' to Jacques Loew, Mission to the Poorest [New York: Sheed and Ward, 1950], vi).

19. Catherine Masson, 'Ruptures et renouveaux', 82. 'Even in Rome some like Msgr Tardini, a close collaborator of Pius XII, deplored the inopportune approach of those decisions, noting that the situation was complicated by the Pope being sick' (Catherine Masson, 'Ruptures et renouveaux', 82).

20. Leprieur, *Quand Rome condamne*, 313. Loew mentioned that he found in Rome misunderstanding and misrepresentation about everything in the French church (Leprieur, 403).

In the issue of *La Vie intellectuelle* for February, 1954, leading Dominican theologians supported the movement. The historian and pastoral theologian Henri-M Féret, OP, came to see the conflict as grounded in a sociological struggle between the church's hierarchy accustomed to full control and a church-in-mission among the working class.[21] Congar wrote:

> I am often asked if there is a line between the priest-workers and the Dominicans. Is the connection accidental or is there a real connection? I think that the connection is found in the anxiety of 'Rome' over all that does not please them and all that they see as dangerous. Others may find more connections.[22]

While the priest-workers were being disciplined, French theologians, particularly Dominicans, would be removed from office. The Master of the Dominican Order Emmanuel Suarez flew to Paris and addressed the Dominicans assembled there: 'We must give some satisfaction to the Holy See, signs of obedience and of discipline. Then after a while all this will be forgotten.' The Master General removed all three provincials, the provincial directors of studies for the three provinces, the director of the publishing house, and theology professors: those actions were utterly contradictory to the Dominican tradition of democracy.[23] Joseph Robert, OP, wrote: 'I am troubled by the possible motives for this condemnation. We have been attacked and slandered. To me it seems terrible that the church, or rather certain authorities in the church, accept this—and accept it repeatedly.'[24]

Withdrawing from factory employment, Loew and others continued their new forms of community life and ministry in factory neighborhoods and saw nothing disobedient in seeking to support themselves by some form of labor. So priest-workers still lived from working—although not in factories—and they were convinced that in spite of the problems the movement had provided an effective pastoral ministry. 'Of course a priest

---

21. Leprieur, *Quand Rome condamne,* 406.
22. Congar cited in Leprieur, *Quand Rome condamne,* 765; see Yves Congar, Jacques Loew, René Voillaume, *À temps et à contretemps: Retrouver dans l'Église le visage de Jésus-Christ* (Paris: Cerf, 1969).
23. The Dominican provincial of Paris wrote: 'I cannot help being shocked and scandalized that Rome is condemning and penalizing members of a religious Order without giving them a hearing' (Leprieur, 413).
24. Leprieur, *Quand Rome condamne,* 413.

can belong to a trade union', he maintained. 'This does not mean selling out your priesthood.' His ministry made him suspect to some bishops, and his superiors asked for more involvement with the externals of Dominican life.[25] He was told to stay away from the younger members of the Province, away from the house of formation, and to wear his habit more often.[26] Other priest-workers, however, kept their factory jobs and argued with church authorities.[27] By July, 1954, Loew had the permission of the Archbishop of Marseilles to continue his ministerial community.

Loew gave countless talks and wrote many books and articles. The early descriptions in *Les Dockers de Marseille* (1944) and *Un Mission Prolétarienne* (1946) were followed by his diary of turbulent years *Journal d'une Mission Ouvrière, 1941–1959*, struggling to find new ways of thinking about workers' problems and workers' faith.[28] As the years passed, he published a number of books on spirituality, often the results of retreats given around Europe: already in the 1950s some of his writings appeared in English translations.[29]

In his work on pastoral theology from 1964 what stands out are the person called to evangelization, the call itself, an expanding presence of the Lord in society, and the multiple ways in which grace touches non-believers.[30] False forms of religion aim at externals: they resemble a cult and they fashion a sect. Today the need is for a 'cult of truth' and a community respecting all people in an attention to the 'present instant'. Jesus calls people to ministry by baptism, religious vows, and ordination. Since these vocations are complementary, today's collective form of ministry,

25. Leprieur, *Quand Rome condamne*, 99.
26. Leprieur, *Quand Rome condamne*, 99.
27. Leprieur, *Quand Rome condamne*, 275–78.
28. (Paris: Cerf, 1959).
29. Si vous saviez le don de Dieu (Paris: Cerf, 1958); Dans la nuit j'ai cherché (Paris: Cerf, 1969). There are reflections on great mystics in Prière à l'école des grands priants (Paris: Fayard, 1975) and La Vie à l'écoute des grands priants (Paris: Fayard-Mame, 1986). Writings translated into English include: Face to Face with God, The Bible's Way to Prayer (Mahwah: Paulist, 1977); The Love We Forget (1958). In 1989 the Dominican received the Grand Prix Catholique de Littérature. For American priests amid workers' lives, in film and reality, see James T Fisher, 'The Priest in the Movie: On the Waterfront as Historical Theology', in Gary Macy, editor, Theology and the New Histories (Maryknoll: Orbis, 1999), 167–85.
30. Comme s'il voyait l'invisible: Un portrait de l'apôtre d'aujourd'hui (Paris: Cerf, 1964). [English As if He Had Seen the Invisible: a Portrait of the Apostle Today (Notre Dame: Fides Press, 1967)].

the team, seeks out all those called in various ways and enables them to call others. 'What is lacking to the apostle today for accomplishing the mission is not contact with people . . . but the enthusiasm of certitude, of a conviction. God can cover the world with his presence through everything that happens to us; all he needs from us is a bit of faith.'[31]

From Condemnation to Expansion

A retreat he gave in August of 1955 was attended by a large number of priests and young people interested in or committed to linking theology and ministry in society. Jacques Loew had been entertaining the idea of founding a religious congregation, a secular institute taking on a missionary form suited to today's societies.[32] In those weeks the Mission Ouvrière Saints Pierre et Paul (MOPP) was founded to evangelise the working class. In 1956, the members held a study-retreat at the Trappist Abbey of Citeaux, the first of many meetings for group formation held at the original abbey of the Cistercians during the following years.[33] The Archbishop of Aix-en-Provence recognised the new community officially, and they began to publish their newsletter *Journal d'une Mission Ouvrière*. Loew's formula remained much the same. 'A life shared in all respects with that of the district. Before you can be a "good neighbor" you must first be a neighbor . . . The organization of a center for material services [was] in order gradually to improve social conditions and raise the standard of living.'[34] Loew's ministerial community received approbation by Rome as an apostolic institute of diocesan format in 1965. With the approval of his Dominican superiors and the understanding of his brother friars, he left the Order of Preachers to belong to the new group.

In the 1960s the congregation established missions in the region of the Sahara and in Brazil. Loew described the origins and early history of this new kind of evangelical community in *Les Cieux Ouverts: Chronique de la Mission Ouvrière Saints-Pierre-et-Paul, 1955–1970.*[35] He became active in

---

31. *Les Cieux ouverts: Chronique de la Mission ouvrière Saints-Pierre-et-Paul, 1955-1970*, (Paris: Cerf, 1971), 85.

32. Leprieur, 462; see G Defois, *Vulnérable et passionante Église: Les enjeux d'aujourd'hui* (Paris: Cerf, 1977).

33. During the week after Easter of 1964, I was at Citeaux and took part in the Eucharist celebrated by Jacques Loew and his team who were there on a study retreat.

34. *Mission to the Poorest*, 57.

35. *Les Cieux ouverts: Chronique de la Mission ouvrière Saints-Pierre-et-Paul 1955–1970* (Paris: Cerf, 1971).

Brazilian communities in 1968, intending to spend the rest of his life in
the shanty towns of São Paulo. However, by 1969 he was back in Europe,
establishing the School of Faith in Fribourg, Switzerland. It was one of
the first theological schools where theology encountered new ministries.
The number of young men and women interested in lay ministry to the
poor was growing, and the school received several hundred students each
year. In February, 1970, at the invitation of Pope Paul VI he preached the
Lenten retreat in the Vatican: his theme was 'This Jesus Whom They Call
the Christ'.[36] There were further foundations in Montreal, Tokyo, Paris,
and Salvador de Bahia, Brazil. In August, 1973 he resigned from leading
the new congregation and was replaced by Michel Cuénot. Throughout
his energetic and varied life Loew remained committed to his mission as
a priest at the service of the poor.

At Vatican II there had been discussions over the rehabilitation of the
movement of priest-workers. The document *Presbyterorum Ordinis* spoke
of a variety of ways of being a priest and of new adaptations of the ordained ministry of the presbyter to society. Documents like *Gaudium et
Spes* offered broader theologies of the relationship of church to world, a
backdrop for a variety of ways by which the church's ordained and baptismal ministries serve society.[37] Around the world there was a move away
from seeing the priest as an isolated sacral figure for whom society and
work were rather alien to seeing him as a coordinator and sacrament of
ministry and mission. The priest-workers had played an important role in
the emergence of a broader theology of the church in the world.

Experts see the condemnation of the movement of less than a hundred people to have been a severe shock for the pastoral life of the French
church in the twentieth century. It halted a dynamic producing much
good, it identified the church with blind obedience to uninformed ecclesiastics, and it rejected society and history. Jacques Julliard, an expert in
French sociology, concluded:

> The reasons for the Roman actions are to be found first in
> different ideas of the priesthood itself. What is a priest? A
> professional administering the sacraments, a man apart? Or,
> on the other hand, a witness of Jesus Christ in a milieu which

---

36. *Ce Jésus qu'on appelle Christ (Mt. 1, 16): Retraite au Vatican 1970* (Paris: Fayard, 1970).
37. See Yves Congar, M Peuchmaurd, editors, *L'Église dans le monde de ce Temps: Constitu-
    tion pastorale 'Gaudium et Spes'* (Paris: Cerf, 1967) 3 volumes [*Unam Sanctam* 65a–c].

ignores Jesus? Also one cannot separate this theological debate from its political and intellectual context at that time. We are in the cold war; Pius XII lived in the fear of priests being contaminated by Marxists. Something similar happens twenty-five years later in Latin America with theologies of liberation.[38]

The following words from Loew speaking in the early 1940s anticipate Latin American base communities and North American ecclesial lay ministry.[39]

> Missionary priests will be at pains to mingle with the community of the faithful. They will be a small group united as a working team within the parish. Their great work will be gradually to re-form the inhabitants of the parish area into a spiritual community, and the church into a center where this community can meet. They will not hesitate to say Mass in this courtyard or that living room, so that more believers and non-believers will be drawn to the common house of the faithful. The priests cannot do everything in the parishes. Along with the lay missionaries of social reform and the missionary priests will come other missionaries . . . residing in the district, single or married.[40]

The reality and challenge of the worker-ministers—sisters and laity as well as priests—went further than the parishes of French Catholics; it had to do with the theological self-understanding of the church's mission and with the liberation of religious life and the priesthood.

A Contemplative Mission

As old age approached Jacques Loew did not draw back from mission and ministry; he went to Zaire, Poland, Canada, Hungary, Japan, and the Ivory Coast. He remained a member of MOPP after he gave up the direc-

---

38. Leprieur, 767. "Not 100 priest-workers worked in factories before 1954, and only eleven of them were Dominicans. Thirty years later there are 450 priest-workers in France" (Engel, "Bürgerliche Priester – Proletarische Priester," 144).
39. See D Barbé, *Demain, les communautés de base* (Paris: Cerf, 1970).
40. *Mission to the Poorest*, 121.

tion of the school in Fribourg. Then, in 1982, he retired to the Trappists at Citeaux, to begin a further journey, a monastic one lasting almost twenty years. 'For my retirement I wanted to share in a life of silence and prayer', he said. In 1986, he moved to an eremitical community of nuns at Tamié near Albertville in the Alps with a view of Mont Blanc. He went in 1990 to live with a community of Trappist nuns at Echourgnac in Périgord. He died there on the 14th of February 1999.

Jacques Loew's person and intuition were stronger than the controls of a rigid ecclesiastical system: stronger than the strictures of feudalism, the externals of the Baroque, and the hostilities of modernity. Reading pages written by him one finds realism and brevity; reading about him one senses the smells of people and work. His theology of hard experience is a refreshing alternative to the refined sensibilities, neo-medieval and aesthetic, of others speaking of faith at the same time.[41]

Jacques Loew was an activist and a contemplative. He was creating ministries as he contemplated the presence of God in the world. He was praying and he was loading ships.

---

41. A novelistic portrayal of the emergence of priest-workers published in France in 1966 is Jean Sulivan, *Eternity, My Beloved* (St Paul: River Boat Books, 1998).

Chapter 6

Pierre-André Liégé: Developing Pastoral Theology

Americans who studied theology in Paris in the 1960s returned home with exciting stories about a professor named Pierre-André Liégé. He had fresh ideas and a gift for teaching, developing new approaches for both youth and adult faith formation. Like the other French Dominicans, he had a dynamic vision of the church that contrasted with the clerical model that prevailed in the United States until Vatican II. Liégé was experienced in pastoral ministry and he was sought after as a preacher and retreat master. He often worked with pastors and parishes to help them improve their programs.

For about thirty years before he died in 1979 at the age of 58, Liégé was something of a pastoral whirlwind in France. His career is interesting for two reasons. First, he contributed to the evolution of catechetics and pastoral theology emerging as a potent force in Europe in the 1950s and 60s; and second, the issues that he focused on are still vital for church life today. Liégé saw that the church had to relate to secularised society and to teach in terms that ordinary people could understand. He also knew that the faith had to engage people in their ordinary situations in order to attract the apostolic talents of all the faithful. Like Lebret and Loew, he wanted the church's missionary impulse to reach all its members.

He illustrates how the church adapts its self-understanding as its mission evolves. Liégé played an important role both in the Dominican Order and in the French church, helping to redefine their theology and pastoral life. He also was drawn into the work of Vatican II, going to Rome as the assistant to two French bishops, and he had a hand both in the preparation of council documents and in the seminars and panels that explained the theological issues under debate to the bishops.

Like Chenu and Congar, Liégé was also the target of Vatican surveil-
lance and of denunciations to the Holy See. Along with his great mentors
he was identified with Le Saulchoir and its dialogue with contemporary
culture. He became a notable voice in the church's presence among the
working class, intellectuals, and youth. That was sufficient to arouse suspicions in Rome. Unlike his mentors, Liégé was never suspended from his
teaching or sent into exile. But he had to endure the annoyance of inter-
rogations and accusations over many years.

From a Rural Background

Pierre Liégé was born on the 22nd of June 1921 in the Burgundy hill country in a village called Coiffy-le-Bas. His father was a horse dealer and his
mother a school teacher. Pierre was the oldest of four children; he had
two brothers and a sister. Both his brothers went into the horse business
with their father. No one in his family had any particular attachment to
the church.

Later in life, Pierre's colleagues described him as "earthy" and attribut-
ed his ease with people to his rural background. He could easily reach out
to people and his self-confidence was one of his great personal resources.
His mother Suzanne, the village schoolmistress, was his first teacher. As
he grew up, he attended Lycées in Langres and in Montebéliard and was
a fine student in both. At sixteen, he joined the upper level of the Scouts
called the *Routiers* (meaning those *en route*). This branch of the Scouts
later became very important for him.[1]

Scouting was also important for his vocation, since scouting in France
was connected with adolescent spiritual formation as well as with youth-
ful quest for adventure. A priest, probably his scout chaplain, inspired
Pierre to take the Catholic faith seriously. He went into the seminary at
Montmagny near Paris, and at age seventeen entered the novitiate of the
Dominican Order in Amiens in 1938. He had first explored the Benedic-

---

1. See *Pierre-André Liégé: Témoin de Jésus-Christ* (Paris: Cerf, 1980), a volume of reminis-
    cences and tributes to Liégé published shortly after his death (further references to this
    work will be indicated as *PAL*). I have depended upon two PhD dissertations treating
    Liégé's life and work: Nicholas Bradbury, *The Pastoral Theology of Pierre-André Liégé: a
    Critical and Comparative Study in Pastoral and Practical Theology* (Cardiff University
    [England], 2008) unpublished, and Frank C Sokol, *The Mission of the Church and the
    Nature of Catechesis in the Writings of Pierre-André Liégé (1921–1979)*, (Washington
    DC: Catholic University of America, 1983), published by University Microfilms Inter-
    national. Bradbury had the advantage of interviewing Liégé's sister Nelly at her home,
    from whom he learned many of the details of his life as a youth and as an adult.

tine Order. However, Liégé was advised that the Dominicans would be a better fit for him.[2] He was a thinker, and in France the Dominicans were in the forefront of Catholic intellectual life.

In the novitiate, Pierre took the religious name André. The following year, he took his first vows and was sent to Le Saulchoir to begin his studies. He found there an intellectual community that included Chenu, Congar, and other professors of philosophy, theology, Scripture and medieval studies who were among the leading lights of the French church. They considered St Thomas Aquinas a dialogue partner for the contemporary concerns of church and society. Chenu's historical perspective, mentioned before, saw St Thomas's thought not so much as a message from the past as a resource for the present. Liégé learned to apply the principles of his theology to the social and historical experience of his own time.

All of this pointed Liégé in the direction of pastoral theology. Even with its technical sophistication, his Le Saulchoir education did not distance him from the mission of the church and the life of its people. Liégé's characteristic theological preoccupation became making the church fully alive in its present circumstances.

Yves Congar was Liégé's professor both before and after Congar's years away at war (1939–45). From Congar, Liégé absorbed the idea of the importance of understanding the church not in institutional terms, but as a living mystery of sacramental life and holiness. From Congar he also took the themes of the apostolic vocation of the laity and the transformation of all the faithful into likeness to Christ by grace. These were the seeds of what Liégé would later call 'Christian adulthood'.

While pursuing the ordinary course of studies, Liégé also prepared a license in philosophy at the Sorbonne. He was chosen for the lectorate in theology (a degree within the Dominican Order) that would allow him to teach other friars. In June 1944, he was ordained a priest at the chapel of Le Saulchoir.

Beginning in the autumn of 1945, Liégé and Congar became faculty colleagues at Le Saulchoir, and they collaborated on books, articles, and conferences even as they became friends and co-workers. Congar once described Liégé as 'the best of my disciples'.[3] Liégé benefitted from Congar's mentoring as he shaped his own career. In general, they both conceived of their personal work as serving the common interests of the team of scholars who made up the faculty of Le Sauchoir.

2.　Bradbury, *The Pastoral Theology of Pierre-André Liégé*, 53.
3.　François Coudreau, 'L'acte catéchétique', in *PAL*, 128.

In 1948–1949, Liégé went to the University of Tübingen to study with Franz-Xaver Arnold, a noted professor of moral and pastoral theology, from whom he learned about 'kerygmatic theology' and 'pastoral theology', already influential in Germany and Austria.[4] Kerygmatic theology aimed to bring theology into contact with the concerns of lay people in the world. Recognising the need for an adult catechesis for the laity, especially for those working in the sciences and the professions, kerygmatic theology searched out the fundamental message of the New Testament (in Greek, the *kerygma*) as the foundation for a penetrating faith. Rather than stressing a systematic theology based on abstract ideas, it immersed believers in biblical texts that proclaimed the first and foundational preaching of the early church. This approach was developing at a time when Catholics were for the first time becoming familiar and comfortable with reading the scriptures on their own. So kerygmatic theology had the advantage of directing the lay faithful to immediate, personal contact with the word of God.

In Germany, two figures were attracting a great deal of attention in theology: Karl Adam, a professor at Tübingen and a religious writer with wide appeal, and Romano Guardini in Munich, lecturing on new directions in spirituality and liturgy. Liégé adopted Guardini's concern for the relation of theology to culture, especially Guardini's conviction that tension between theology and culture is positive and creative, and that both poles must be taken seriously on their own terms. This remained a principle for Liégé for the rest of his life. His theology is substantially a theology of culture.

Returning to Le Saulchoir in 1949, Liégé became part of one of the chief centers of theological renewal in Europe. Congar was a pioneer in ecclesiology and ecumenism; others were leaders in the liturgical movement, like A-M Roguet and later Pierre-Marie Gy; and exegetes who had trained at the École Biblique in Jerusalem were working on the innovative Jerusalem Bible, like Thomas-Georges Chifflot and André Dubarle. Their theology was both pastoral and practical in the spirit of Chenu who summarised the ethos of the school this way: 'Any theology worthy of the name is a spirituality that has found rational instruments [tools for reflection] equal to its religious experience.'[5] They shared a common interest in

---

4.   See Bradbury, *The Pastoral Theology of Pierre-André Liégé*, 56f.
5.   M-D Chenu, *Une école de théologie: Le Saulchoir* (Kain-lez-Tournai: Le Saulchoir, 1937), 75. See a description of Le Saulchoir in the essay on Père Chenu in this book.

the spiritual and theological evolution taking place in the French church. Their research and theology were linked to this pastoral renaissance and guided it.

Some Strange Interests

Two areas of interest for Liégé may appear a bit strange. The first was his involvement in the French scouting movement, and the second his role for two decades as a professor of preaching. Neither of these would have been considered worthy occupations for a scholar in those days, although in both cases he sharpened his skills as a thinker and had substantial influence upon others.

In Catholic France priest chaplains for the scouts were normal. Despite the French Revolution and the secular (perhaps even anticlerical) character of the French government, until the 1970s the majority of French people were baptised and thought of themselves as Catholics. When the scout movement took root in France, naturally the ideal of the Boys Scouts' founder, the Englishman Baden-Powell, was transformed by French culture. The scouts' goal of implanting traditional values in youth included religious values, which in France were Catholic values.

In 1920, a Jesuit named Père Jacques Sevin founded the scout movement in France as a type of cultural and religious formation, offering opportunities not only for civic growth and community building, but also for religious formation. So when Liégé joined the scouts in 1937, his troop or *clan* had a Catholic priest chaplain. Chaplains realised that their connection with bright and active adolescents was a rare opportunity for engaging their interest and attention at an impressionable moment in their lives. Scout chaplaincies were serious business.

Decades later, when another Jesuit, Père Doncoeur, retired as chaplain to the 'Clan Routier' attached to the École Polytechnique in Paris (a prestigious school for France's most gifted students), Liégé took his place. That began a ten-year investment on his part as chaplain, first for the Polytechnique and later (1951 to 1957) as national chaplain to the *Routiers de France* (with members between seventeen and twenty years of age). Liégé played this role while becoming more involved in theological teaching (at Le Saulchoir and later at the Institut Catholique in Paris). He loved contact with young people.[6]

---

6. For Liégé and his scout connections, see the new study by Gérard Reynal, *Pierre-André Liégé: Un itinéraire théologique au milieu du XXe siècle* (Paris: Cerf, 2010). Cf P Rendu,

In 1953, Jean-Pierre Jossua as a young man went with Père Liégé on the huge Easter pilgrimage of *Routier* scouts to Vezelay. He describes Liégé's ability not only to engage and excite this huge crowd of young people, but also his charism for suffusing the pilgrimage with a sense of joy and celebration. Jossua remarks, 'It was an Easter Vigil of unforgettable luminosity'.[7] Jossua later became an esteemed Dominican theologian and writer who freely acknowledges Liégé's influence in his own life.

Liégé wrote over fifty articles for scouting journals as catechesis for young people. He roused the faith in the young people with whom he worked, preached, and recreated. His chaplaincy also gave him a chance to test ideas from the biblical, liturgical and catechetical renewal. Scouting was a crucible for his pastoral thinking. As he tried to translate the new theology into language that young adults could understand, this paid off in his writing and teaching.

The second unlikely interest was Liégé's role as professor of preaching at Le Saulchoir. Odd as it may seem, Liégé was the first professor of preaching in this theology school for 'preachers'. Until the 1950s, there had been no preaching even at Sunday Mass at Le Saulchoir, even though it was a community of more than a hundred friars. They thought that an elaborate liturgy would distract them from study time. This attitude changed for many reasons, including the liturgical movement that saw the homily not as an ornament but an integral part of the Mass. As professors also became more involved pastorally, a new prior wanted preaching to play its proper role in the life of the community.

Liégé was an unusually able preacher. He was given charge of training the student friars. Each week two student friars would preach practice homilies before the student community in chapel, and then another student (chosen on the spot) was asked to critique the preachers. 'That seemed a sure way to see that everyone paid attention', remarked Patrick Jaquemont, the friar who succeeded him in the job. Liégé sat in front taking notes and he gave his own critique, which was characteristically challenging and thorough. As Jacquemont remarked, Liégé was brutally frank but equally clear about his criteria for successful preaching. The students learned from him and appreciated his ideas.[8]

'Le Père Liégé et la Route', in *PAL*, 40f.
7.   Jean-Pierre Jossua, 'Une foi de chair et de sang', in *PAL*, 28.
8.   Patrick Jacquemont, 'Partager la passion du prêcher', in *PAL*, 70.

Once a semester, Liégé also gave a lecture at the Saulchoir on preaching in the context of pastoral theology. He treated the history and theology of preaching, the nature of the homily, the various contexts for preaching, as well as methods for oral expression and sermon composition. His emphasis was on the theology of the word of God and the power of sacred Scripture. Liégé spoke of *paranetic* preaching—preaching that exhorts and invites people to live a Christian life. He could inculturate the biblical message to make it feel like a word for here and now. For Liégé, there should always be a link between the ministry of the word and building up the church.[9] For that to happen, preaching needed to be clear, practical, and realistic.

Real Gospel, Real Theology

In the 1950s Liégé was preoccupied with 'demystifying' false images of God. Bultmann's theology of demythologising was current at the time, and in all likelihood Liégé was influenced by Bultmann's terminology. But he also knew that most adults held on to infantile notions of God that ill suited their adult posture in the world. Therefore this demystification of irrational fear, of a floating sense of guilt, and of images of God as an arbitrary judge had a missionary dimension. Those false images had to be disposed of, if people were going to see and hear Jesus Christ for what he is, the revelation of God's mercy and the source of human solidarity with God. The preacher must be critical or even challenging when the true character of the gospel is at stake or is being held hostage by superstition or moralism.

In 1961, Liégé preached a series of Lenten sermons at Saint Sulpice in Paris that exemplified this. He spoke of the 'contagion' of the gospel, its capacity to change lives by being transmitted through new ways of living. Christian life becomes contagious by being passed on through the integrity that the faithful live in the midst of others. However, Christians must be in contact with their contemporaries. So Liégé explained that 'when the church finds a new way of being in the world, it can lead the world to a recovery of Christian faith'. Profound catechesis and good preaching can imitate Jesus in commanding hearers to 'get up and walk'. Many people felt that Liégé succeeded in doing just that.[10]

---

9. See Bradbury, *The Pastoral Theology of Pierre-André Liégé*, 64–67.
10. Jacquemont, 'Partager la passion du prêcher', in *PAL*, 72.

The Institut Catholique and Liégé's Catechetical Institute

In 1950, France was at an epochal turning point. The church was taking initiatives to reach out to workers and youth and was reaping the fruits of the biblical and liturgical movements, creating a new awareness of the richness of the gospel. Writers and pastors, theologians and bishops were talking, dreaming, and working together. Roman church authorities, however, incited by theologians of the right, grew suspicious and harshly intolerant of innovations either in theological writing or in pastoral initiatives. They were on the lookout for problems to condemn.

In 1950 Pope Pius XII published his encyclical *Humani Generis* to halt innovations. It cast a shadow over the use of historical method in theology and over pastoral experimentation. Two elements touched on by the encyclical are noteworthy here. First, the pope insisted that Thomism is the only true Christian philosophy and theology, and second, he claimed that when a pope pronounces upon a controverted issue, it may no longer be regarded as a matter of free debate among theologians or among the faithful.[11] So, in France at least, 1950 was the moment when the post-war Catholic revival collided with the reaction of Vatican authorities.

There was still momentum in the French pastoral renaissance, however, and one example is the bishops' invitation to Sulpician seminary professor, François Coudreau, SS, to create a chair in catechetics at the Institut Catholique (the Catholic university) of Paris.[12] Along with Joseph Colomb, another Sulpician, Coudreau had been creating new, pastorally sensitive books and programs for teaching the faith to both children and adults. Previous 'catechisms' had been typically in a question-and-answer

---

11. Pope Pius XII, *Humani Generis* (1950)—*cf* www.vatican.va §20: 'Nor must it be thought that what is expounded in Encyclical Letters does not of itself demand consent, since in writing such Letters the Popes do not exercise the supreme power of their Teaching Authority. For these matters are taught with the ordinary teaching authority, of which it is true to say: 'He who heareth you, heareth me'; and generally what is expounded and inculcated in Encyclical Letters already for other reasons appertains to Catholic doctrine. But if the Supreme Pontiffs in their official documents purposely pass judgment on a matter up to that time under dispute, it is obvious that that matter, according to the mind and will of the Pontiffs, cannot be any longer considered a question open to discussion among theologians.' It is noteworthy that nowhere in the sixteen documents of Vatican II is this claim to a quasi-definitive force of papal statements reiterated.
12. For the details of this fascinating initiative, see Bradbury, *The Pastoral Theology of Pierre-André Liégé*, 67f.

form that required rote learning and discouraged creative reflection or adaptations to local circumstances. By contrast, the new catechetical movement dwelt upon questions that many people were asking before providing answers. Baptised adults needed to own their faith, if the faith was to become the wellspring of their life and work. Baptism was beginning to be recognised once again as a life-long project.

The catechetical movement in France is interesting. For years Père Colomb, SS, (1902–1979) had taught in the Sulpician seminaries of Lyons and Autun. In 1945, he was commissioned by Cardinal Gerlier of Lyons to establish a center for training catechists in his new methods of pedagogy. These were mostly religious sisters or lay people who assisted priests in giving religious instruction in the parishes. After founding his school for professional catechists in Lyons, Colomb produced his popular *Catéchisme Progressif*. It was progressive in developing approaches geared to the growing abilities of children and adolescents as they matured. Colomb's catechism was a resounding success. There were sixteen editions of it printed between 1945 and 1947, including materials addressed to adults and especially to parents. Naturally, then, Coudreau had Colomb in mind as a collaborator for his catechetical program at the Institut Catholique. Colomb's approach had already demonstrated its effectiveness and Coudreau and Colomb both had the support not only of Cardinal Gerlier, but of other French bishops as well.

In August 1950, Coudreau went to a Jesuit retreat house near Montauban for a month-long retreat for which Yves Congar had been slated as the principal presenter. For some reason, Congar was unable to come and he asked his colleague Liégé to take his place. Coudreau's first instinct was to drop out of the program if Congar was not going to be there, but he was persuaded by the center's director to give Liégé a chance. The director told Coudreau that Congar had said that Liégé had been his best student. So Coudreau stayed on and discovered that Liégé's lectures on God's word as a divine summons to the whole of humanity provided insights into a psychology of faith and conversion that helped him greatly.

Coudreau felt as though Liégé were showing him the direction that his program at the Institut Catholique should take. He was impressed and moved. Even though his invitation from the bishops to create a chair in catechetics still was a secret, Coudreau's confidence in Liégé was so great that he shared his news with him. Liégé was exhilarated and told Coudreau: 'This is decisive—a major event for the church. If you want me to,

I'll join you!'[13] Liégé, who knew the Institut Catholique quite well, was also more than a little surprised. This kind of program was a great 'novelty' in the Roman sense of the word and would likely provoke a ruinous reaction from the Vatican. Nonetheless, Coudreau and Liégé undertook what would become an enduring legacy in pastoral education.

In October the professors of the Institut Catholique refused to accept the proposed chair of catechetics, claiming that if it were about the content of the faith, this was already adequately treated by the faculty of theology; and if it were about pedagogy, that had no place in a school of theology. The rector, Msgr Blanchet, sidestepped the impasse by replacing the chair of catechetics with an *Institut Supérieur d'Enseignement Catéchétique* (ISEC), meaning a graduate program in religious education housed in a separate department.[14]

This ISEC soon became well known. Coudreau taught the education courses, Liégé taught kerygmatic theology, and there were courses in developmental psychology and the history of catechetics, the latter taught by the Jesuit Jean Daniélou. Liégé's classroom was jammed with students and visitors. Coudreau admitted that Liégé was the one who had the imagination and skill to create the structures and courses needed to make the institute a success. Soon ISEC had students applying from all over the world.

Liégé's course was a sensation. Just the name kerygmatic theology was a novelty in France. Like Colomb with his catechisms, Liégé recognised that the Bible had to be the foundation for any genuine catechesis. Beginning with the *kergma* (foundational proclamation) of the apostles also made it clear that theology had developed and does develop according to the culture and pastoral needs of changing times. This introduced an element of freedom and creativity into the pastoral mission of handing on what the church has received from the apostles.

As Nicholas Bradbury writes:

> Tackling head on the problems involved in thinking about Religious Education, Liégé began to show that the triple renewal in biblical, liturgical and pedagogic studies then under way had radical consequences far beyond their usefulness for a new catechism . . . He called for *theological renewal*

---

13. Coudreau, 'L'acte catéchétique', in *PAL*, 129.
14. Bradbury, *The Pastoral Theology of Pierre-André Liégé*, 67–72.

based precisely on confronting it with praxis, with issues and questions of current concern.[15]

Further, the critical audience for such catechesis was clearly first of all adults, not children.

The catechetical institute linked university level theology with concrete pastoral praxis. Liégé insisted that the students must have pastoral placements where they would be supervised in applying what they were learning by teaching in schools, parishes, and other church institutions; and he devised the norms and methods for these placements and their evaluation. Theological reflection about their teaching experiences, about the needs and responses of their pupils, and also about their own reactions became a standard element of the program. In this way integrating doctrine, theological reflection, and the insights from the social sciences became not a mix of diverse elements standing side by side but a single synthetic experience.

The synergy of two elements, theology and praxis, constituted a new reality for theological education that the institute called "catechetics." Not only was this *practical* theology in the most genuine sense, but it also yielded insight into the task of evangelizing the faithful. In those early days, some of the young clergy returned to the Institut Catholique precisely in order to learn this new method. As one of them put it, 'I had to work hard in that program because I wanted to make sense of what effective pastoral ministry would look like if the different disciplines we were learning fit together with Scripture and Tradition.'[16] Many pastors realised that the seminary courses that they had taken didn't go nearly far enough to prepare them to enter into a dialogue of faith with people in this postwar pastoral scene. They were hungry for insights about how to be better preachers and catechists.

However, difficulties arose with Rome just as this experiment of the Institut Catéchétique was becoming stable and achieving success. There had been rumbles of discontent from Rome concerning Colomb's catechisms and his center in Lyons. Right wing clergy and laity had denounced him to the Holy See, and there had already been a condemnation from the Holy Office of one of his catechisms. In the summer of 1957, the cardinal

---

15. Bradbury, *The Pastoral Theology of Pierre-André Liégé*, 86.
16. Michel Duhamel, cited in Bradbury, *The Pastoral Theology of Pierre-André Liégé*, 69.

in charge of overseeing the church's doctrinal orthodoxy, Alfredo Otta-
viani, called for the dismissal of both Colomb and Coudreau from their
roles as professors and educational administrators.[17] Cardinal Gerlier and
Archbishop de Provenchères, who was executive director of religious education for the French bishops, both interceded with the Vatican on behalf
of Coudreau and Colomb, but to no effect. Coudreau was forced to resign
from the ISEC and several professors in the Institute were also dismissed
from their posts or reprimanded. Even though Liégé's course on kerygmatic theology was perhaps the most prominent element of the program,
for some reason he himself was not forced to resign. But he was under a
shadow for the rest of his life as far as the Roman Curia was concerned.

It is possible that Coudreau and Colomb both had to resign because
they had been the authors of new catechisms being widely used, while
Liégé himself had not written a catechism. Several bishops also insisted
on the value of Liégé's work for the future of French religious education,
and their support was important. So in the fall of 1957, without his friend
Coudreau and without several former colleagues (including Henri Féret,
OP, who had taught the history of the church in his program), Liégé began
his course on kerygmatic theology in the Institut Catéchétique along the
same lines as before, with students flocking to his classroom.

The Roman Complaints

Unlike Congar, Liégé seems not to have kept a journal, at least not system-
atically. So we owe to Congar's journals a detailed account of Liégé's inter-
actions with the Roman Curia and with the Dominican Master Generals
who enforced the Vatican's decrees. In June, 1953, Liégé was summoned
to Rome, accompanied by his provincial, Père Albert Avril, who had already defended him against denunciations of his teaching and writing by
soliciting support from the rector of the Institut Catholique and members
of the faculty. In Rome, however, Liégé was told by Master General Suarez
that the Holy Office had informed him that there were more than one
hundred denunciations of his work, some coming from bishops. At this
point, after a lengthy discussion, Liégé was warned to be prudent and sent
back to Paris.[18]

---

17. See Bradbury, *The Pastoral Theology of Pierre-André Liégé*, 71f.
18. François Leprieur, *Quand Rome condamne* (Paris: Plon/Cerf, 1989), 35–38.

Two years later in November of 1955, back in Rome again, Liégé reported to Congar about his visit with the new Master General, Michael Browne. The Master General told Liégé that as a theologian he should follow the church's point of view, which is simple, namely, that 'Thomism is the truth; and our only job is to follow, disseminate and integrate the messages that come from the pope'.[19] Master General Browne's warning went further: to talk so much about Eucharistic community, as Liégé did, fails to respect the dignity that Pius XII accorded to private Masses. Further, in Liégé's articles in *La Route, L'Aumônier Scout*, and elsewhere, he does not comment enough about papal teaching. He should be informing people about what the pope says. Further, in speaking about faith, he does so not in the spirit of *Humani Generis* and Vatican I, but in biblical categories. The Master General reproached Liégé for having written that Christ was constituted as Lord by his resurrection and glorification, since Catholics should believe that what makes Christ to be Lord is the hypostatic union. Liégé explained what he had written by referring to Romans and First Peter, but the Master General replied that the authentic meaning of revelation was definitively fixed in scholastic theology, and that is how our theological writings should be phrased.

Finally, the Master General told Liégé that he realised that he was a good religious and that he knew that he had a lot of influence on young people. In fact, Cardinal Marella, the nuncio in France, thought that he had too much influence. Therefore Liégé needed to conform his teaching and writing to the thinking and writings of the pope. In addition, he will have to send everything he writes to the Master General now, so that the Master can help him to correct his ways with paternal advice.[20] The Master General went on to say that it is not just the Dominicans who are the problem. 'The whole of French Catholicism, instead of following exactly what the pope is saying, is daring to think for itself and drawing on sources in contact with dangerous non-Catholic ideologies.'[21] As Congar remarked in his journal in pondering all this, he and Liégé wondered how it could come about that the Roman Curia thinks it can replace the role of the Holy Spirit in the church. Liégé was profoundly discouraged by his interview with the Master General and by the complaints of the Vatican and wanted to retire from his teaching at the Institut Catholique.

---

19. Yves Congar, *Journal d'un théologien 1945-1956* (Paris: Cerf, 2001), 404.
20. Yves Congar, *Journal d'un théologien*, 404–406.
21. Yves Congar, *Journal d'un théologien*, 405–406.

However, over a period of weeks, Cardinal Feltin, the archbishop of Paris, convinced Liégé to continue his teaching at the Institut Catholique. He told Liégé that, if necessary, he personally would intervene with the Holy Father on his behalf. So, back in Paris, Liégé continued his teaching, sobered by this affair and conscious that he was being watched (and often denounced) even if he did not know by whom.

A Theologian of Faith

Liégé returned repeatedly to the issue of what faith means in modern culture. He questioned how someone who is not a mature human being can be a mature Christian. He was reacting to the characteristic passivity and infantile religious understanding that rote religious practice seems not only to tolerate but to encourage. For Liégé there needs to be a proportionate development between human maturity and Christian maturity.

Drawing upon developmental psychology and sociology, Liégé pointed out that adults are persons who have achieved a fundamental unity in their personalities. They are people with experience who are free enough to stand up for what they believe in. They live according to their convictions, owning the decisions that they make. They recognise responsibility not only for their individual acts, but for their developing character. However, many elements in the modern world tend to hinder the development of this kind of maturity. The complexity of modern life, its fast pace, its many avenues of overstimulation, its capacity to manipulate emotions – all these elements maximise the number of maladjusted and neurotic people who are held back from maturing or who are inclined to remain in an infantile or adolescent psychological state. All of this has a lot to do with maturity of faith and Christian life.[22]

Moreover, everyone needs to pass through stages of development in experiencing infancy, youth, maturity, and old age. Each of these stages has religious significance. God is more aware than we are of this developmental trajectory and invites us to pursue its full development. Does that mean, however, that the Christian life can only be led well by completely mature persons? No, there are Christian children and Christian adoles-

22. Liégé's best known work in this vein is *Adultes dans le Christ* (Brussels: La Pensée Catholique, 1958), translated into English by Thomas C Donlan as *Consider Christian Maturity* (Chicago: Priory Press, 1965). I agree with Bradbury that Donlan's translation of the title of this work is unfortunate, given the sustained focus in Liégé's work on the characteristics and tasks of adulthood.

cents as well as Christian adults. But those who remain at a level of human immaturity will lead a life of faith which is only partially transformed and minimally dynamic. Too often Christian teachers or pastors can cheapen religion by adapting it to the sociological conditions in which people find themselves, dragging it down to the level of comforting or utilitarian beliefs, to the level of conventional ethics, or to a practice for individual spiritual comfort. Obviously the gospel cannot let us be content with that.[23]

Luke's Gospel reminds us that Jesus 'went down with [his parents] and came to Nazareth . . . and increased in wisdom and in years and in divine and human favor' (Lk 2:51–52). Unlike the apocryphal gospels, the canonical gospels do not give us a child Jesus who is a miniature adult. They do not conceal Jesus' temptation at the threshold of his entry into public life, but rather show us his steps toward 'growing up'. As Liégé puts it, 'Jesus went to meet his *hour* with the full awareness of an adult'.[24] Jesus Christ is both modelling Christian adulthood for us and sanctifying it. Then from the events of Easter and Pentecost, there came about a revolutionary renewal within the order of human existence. Consequently, as Liégé explains:

> To become a Christian is to enter into this movement with every human potentiality, to allow it to dwell within us, to be guided by its energy, to be vulnerable to its dynamic power. After that happens, life is not what it was before. For this movement is a divine creative initiative—God's bringing about the ultimate divine purpose that was already in view when God first created.[25]

In order for that divine initiative to radically control our lives, we have to become adult both in faith and in life.

This means that Catholic pastors have to assist children and also childish grown-ups to acquire human maturity so that they will become dynamic and apostolic Christian adults. Instead of fearing growth into maturity, with its dangers and its unpredictability, the church ought to

---

23. *Consider Christian Maturity*, 24f. Also, 42–43: 'To those baptised adults who are not really convinced and whose religion has degenerated into formalism, the church must preach conversion in order to draw them out of their childish ways and to introduce them to the fullness of the baptismal life demanded by their age.'
24. *Consider Christian Maturity*, 30.
25. P-A Liégé, *What is Christian Life?* translated by A Manson (New York: Hawthorn, 1961), 9.

encourage it, even if this means that life will be more complicated. To grow up is a risky business, but it is also a great achievement. There are difficulties, setbacks, and limitations in the life of faith; all authentic adult Christians have doubts and challenges, discouragements and fears. But we can't turn the fundamental message of the Gospel into a warning against making mistakes or facing difficulties. Concretely, most baptised adults have to be reminded not to allow their religion to degenerate into formalism. The church has to preach conversion in order to draw chronological adults out of childish ways and introduce them into the responsibility of an apostolic life.[26] This means harder work for pastors and for preachers, because this kind of pastoring can't be done half-heartedly. This is what pastoral work requires, if it is to be realistic.

This fundamental message about the dynamics of an adult faith became an essential part of Liégé's agenda. Increasingly pastors, catechists and the laity recognised the cogency of what he was saying and responded both personally and as ministers to reinvigorate the church's pastoral life. For many parish priests in the 1950s and 60s, Liégé was nothing less than a prophet.

Liégé's theology of the word of God as a living, personal and life-giving link between heaven and earth was a crucial part of this message. This divine word, because it is alive, can speak to us in the present. God's word comes to possess those who respond in faith, transforming them into dynamic personal witnesses who represent the life of the church. For this reason, faith is not essentially understanding ideas, but learning to obey when God speaks to us. Revelation, then, becomes not a literary phenomenon but a personal encounter. So many of these themes, developed by Liégé in the 1950s and 60s, would eventually find expression in Vatican II and be vindicated by the church's magisterium. Like Congar and Lebret, Liégé was helping to prepare dossiers that would enrich the council fathers at Vatican II.

A Place at Vatican II

Liégé considered it a turning point in his life when Pope John XXIII announced his intention to convene an ecumenical council. He had argued for theological renewal for so long despite denunciations and official warnings that the pope's call for *aggiornamento* seemed like the answer

---

26. *Consider Christian Maturity*, chapter 2, 'Achieving Maturity of Faith', 36–55.

to a prayer. At the Council, Liégé became the theological expert of Bishop Schmitt of Metz and Bishop Elchinger of Strasbourg. He was asked to help them particularly with the development of the Constitution on the Church and on the church's mission.[27] Although he was never accepted officially as a *peritus* (a member of the inner circle of advisors), he made significant contributions to the documents. Congar remarked in his Council Journal, "I had already commented several times, at the Council, that the French bishops did not give Fr Liégé the credit that was his due."[28]

Liégé wrote articles about the council for the French Catholic daily *La Croix*, preparing readers for "radical pastoral change" and for a new freedom of expression in presenting Catholic doctrine. Because of his theological research and teaching in catechetics, he was more able than most to address new pastoral developments that emerged at the Council such as the restoration of the catechumenate. Liégé also had close contacts with bishops and with the official theological experts. He lived on the Viale Romania with Hans Küng and a number of French and American bishops.[29] He worked hard for his friends, Bishops Schmitt and Elchinger and for a number of the *periti*, attended a weekly meeting convened by Bishop Elchinger, and got to know and to be trusted by a large circle of influential theologians.

His experience of the council remained a deeply moving memory and the platform on which his future theological work would develop. Bradbury summarises this by saying that Liégé 'wanted an "adult" faith for all, a church made up of people of faith, encouraged by ministers of real service, politically free and unburdened with over-attachment to temporal institutions [and] free to bear witness to Christ. This seemed newly possible to him after the council.'[30] Liégé thought that the council provided the resources needed to develop an adult Catholic practice for the church's laity.

---

27. See Msgr P-J Schmitt, 'La passion de l'Evangile', in *PAL*, 17f. See also L Lemoine, 'Pierre-André Liégé, OP: Témoin et acteur du renouvellement de la théologie catholique autour de Vatican II', in *Faculty of Theology and Religious Sciences, No 118* (Paris: Institut Catholique,1997), 27.

28. Yves Congar, *My Journal of the Council*, translated by Mary John Ronayne, OP, and Cecily Boulding, OP, edited by Denis Minns OP (Adelaide: ATF Press, 2012), 285, entry for March 30, 1963.

29. Jossua, 'Une foi de chair et de sang', in *PAL*, 30.

30. Bradbury, *The Pastoral Theology of Pierre-André Liégé*, 81.

Changes after Vatican II

Although Liégé had taught within the Institut Catéchétique at the Institut Catholique in Paris since 1950, it was not until 1969 that he was invited formally to become a member of the theology faculty. He was well known to his colleagues, and the roster of professors had changed significantly over a period of almost twenty years. His abundant gifts were now apparent to everyone. Further, many who had opposed his catechetical project were no longer at the Institut Catholique.

In 1970, the dean of theology, the distinguished theological historian Louis Cognet, suddenly died. At the beginning of the following academic year, Liégé was unanimously elected to replace him. From then on, Liégé's life was practically consumed by the Institut Catholique, its programs, its politics, and its mission. Now all his hard fought initiatives of the 1950s appeared to be taken for granted. He relished his ability to influence the theological programs at the most important Catholic university in France.

In a few years, the structures of the Institut Catholique were transformed into what came to be called the UER (*Unité d'Enseignement et de Recherche de théologie et de sciences religieuses* – The Faculty for Teaching and Research in Theology and Religious Sciences). Liégé was elected the first director of the UER and helped to shape its programs. Liégé was called upon increasingly for national and episcopal projects, including diocesan synods and the synod of bishops. He also visited Canada and elsewhere for lectures and short courses.

Frank Sokol's 1983 dissertation on Liégé shows that the 1975 Apostolic Exhortation of Pope Paul VI, *Evangelii Nuntiandi*, not only reflects Liégé's writings, but was the fruit of a draft that Liégé wrote.[31] Key phrases that are emblematic of this important papal teaching, 'the church exists in order to evangelize' (§14), 'the church begins by being evangelized herself' (§15), 'the first means of evangelization is the witness of an authentically Christian life' (§41), are vintage Liégé.[32] Jacques Audinet, Liégé's successor at the Institut Catéchétique, wrote that 'it is no secret for anybody that [Liégé] wrote the essential text of *Evangelii Nuntiandi*.'[33] This may be one of his most substantial contributions. Many consider it the most important papal document for ecclesiology following the Council.

31. Sokol, *The Mission of the Church and the Nature of Catechesis,* 211–214.
32. Pope Paul VI, *On Evangelization in the Modern World: Evangelii Nuntiandi* (Vatican City: Libreria Editrice Vaticana, 1975).
33. Sokol, *The Mission of the Church and the Nature of Catechesis,* 247–248: '[C]e n'est un secret pour personne qu'il a rédigé l'essentiel de "Evangelii Nuntiandi".'

Shaping the Future of Pastoral Theology

Liégé's reaction to the narrow position of one of his early collaborators at the Institut Catéchétique prompted his early writings on pastoral theology. Jean Daniélou had taught the history of catechetics in the institute. However, for Daniélou, theology was about texts and their history and had none of the suppleness of Chenu's analogy of pastoral circumstances. If Daniélou situated theology in the church of the past, Liégé was going to situate it in the activities of living people. At the heart of pastoral theology are the actions of ordinary people becoming a conscious embodiment of Christ's presence as a sacrament in the world. The pastoral challenge was to turn kerygmatic theology (a dynamic proclamation of a world changed by Christ) into a liveable set of behaviors that could transform lost souls into the body of Christ.[34]

The challenge was to turn this ultimately practical idea into a scientific university program. To the degree that he did that, he also inaugurated the discipline of pastoral theology in France.[35] He borrowed from Chenu the rich idea that the *praxis ecclesiae*—the church's living organic action—can be considered a *locus theologicus*, that is, a source for theological reflection and understanding. He also claimed that all theology was as concerned with *orthopraxis* (what the church correctly does) as with *orthodoxy* (what the church correctly teaches).

Orthopraxis, called by Liégé *l'agir de l'église* (the church in action), must link questions about the way we live with the way faith governs discipleship. Real theology or catechesis has to be serious about the meaning of life. Otherwise, it will not be up to the job of guiding authentic church life. So Liégé defined pastoral theology (in 1955) as "systematic reflection on the whole of life lived in the church in the process of its self-construction."[36] That is not an easy phrase, but it is dense with meaning. It means paying attention to the understanding and the investment of all the players in the equation–not just the clergy, but the whole people of God. How can they be made to understand that they are as much the church as the pope? How can they be brought to comprehend that their way of living can be as persuasive an argument for the Risen Christ as Sunday preach-

---

34. See G Reynal, *Pierre-André Liégé*.
35. For this section, see Jacques Audinet, 'La théologie pastorale: une ecclésiologie pratique', in *PAL*, 127f.
36. P-A Liégé, 'Pour une théologie pastorale catéchétique', in *Revue des sciences philosophiques et théologiques* 39/1(1955): 5.

ing? How can all of this be articulated in a way that augments rather than diminishes the church's long tradition of sacred teaching?

Liégé tried to recover the combination of biblical and analytical insights that characterised St Augustine's writings. A biblically grounded pastoral theology is as much a need for minimally catechised adults today as it was for the adult converts of Augustine's African church. The church's goal is adult faith, mature Christian life, and responsible gospel freedom. Pastoral theology is scientific reflection upon building up the church to be the people of God.

Liégé described three steps for pastoral theology. First, make Christ's incarnation the focus of salvation, understanding that the church brings about Christ's incarnation in the world today. When we discover the essential meaning of our life by identifying with Christ, we extend the influence of Christ's incarnation into the lives of those with whom we live. Second, understand that revelation takes place inside the story of living persons. Each generation is obliged to create its own expression of the gospel, articulate its own adult faith, and find its own symbols of hope for the kingdom of God. Finally, the church's mission requires that all persons, communities, and generations have to be committed to maintain the apostolic tradition that the church received as its heritage. In this way, God's people, rooted in the apostolic tradition, bear testimony to the faith when they come together to celebrate the Eucharist.[37] Every Christian has a vocation to an apostolic life.[38]

Pastoral theology aims to fashion an apostolic people of God who participate in Christ's three-fold mission as prophet, priest, and Lord of creation. Permanent formation—adult catechesis—is irreplaceable for bringing about mature understanding and for marshalling the energies of a Christian society that is apostolic in every part. For the faithful who are charged with the transformation of the world, grace must be ordinary, discerned as present but hidden in every dimension of social life.

After Vatican II, Liégé was even more conscious of the number of Christians who have never been sufficiently catechised or never grasped the meaning of the church. With them in mind, he explained that everyone possesses a kind of preamble to faith as part of their human hunger

---

37. P-A Liégé, 'Pour une théologie pastorale catéchétique', 6-7.
38. See Vatican II's 'Decree on the Apostolate of Lay People', §2 as well as its 'Decree on the Ministry and Life of Priests', §2: 'There is no such thing as a member who does not have a share in the mission of the whole body.'

for meaning. We all have a readiness for the kerygma based on our life experience of searching for justice and love. Such dispositions prepare us to be open to the grace of the living God.[39] However, the church has to learn again how to communicate its message and abandon its arrogance, imperialism, and self-complacency. That requires a church that is poor, tolerant, and friendly: a church that does not have a reputation for condemning whatever doesn't fit its customary habits.

In the eyes of many, the official church understands neither contemporary culture nor the non-western world. It is over-institutionalised, over-centralised, and over-systematised. As a result it doesn't know how to evangelise. The apostolic message should appear as *good news*, if real evangelization is going to take place. Too often, instead of educating, the preacher indoctrinates; instead of offering freedom, he offers constraints. Lived superficially, the Christian life loses its power to electrify others and to manifest grace in ordinary circumstances. Liégé believed that the gospel can turn lives upside. Living an authentic Christian life ought to have a shock value for those who observe it.

Liégé's preoccupation with pastoral theology had begun simply. His experiences at Le Saulchoir with Young Christian Workers, his chaplaincy with the scouts, and his preaching and assistance in parishes put Liégé in touch with creative and committed elements of the French church. He had been living with Dominican colleagues who were immersed not only in the theology of the day, but also in the experiences of workers, priest-workers, communities of the poor, and university students. His pastoral theology had to face up to the consequences of secularisation, dechristianisation, scientific revolutions, and the brutal effects of urbanisation upon large segments of a formerly agricultural population. Too many people felt lost. His pastoral theology hoped to seek and find them.

The pastoral theology that had been taught in seminaries before Vatican II was centered on preparing clerics to follow rubrics and to consult canon law. Its main purpose had been to satisfy the concerns of church authorities to maintain order and custom. By contrast, the goal of the new

---

39. See the letter of Alfonso Nebreda, founder of the East Asian Pastoral Institute in Manila, who remarks that Liégé coined the term *pre-evangelization* in his article on catechesis in the enclyclopedia *Catholicisme*; Nebreda goes on to state that Liégé's writings and influence were crucial not only for the East Asian Pastoral Institute, but for the whole world of missiology and catechesis: Sokol, *The Mission of the Church and the Nature of Catechesis*, 243.

pastoral theology was communication with people in the actual situation of their lives. Liégé worried that the church's ministers had become alienated from their own best instincts by a kind of theological abstraction and formalism. However, by drawing upon biblical, liturgical, and patristic sources, pastoral theology could reconstitute the terrain on which ministry is exercised. Pastoral theology's focus upon an apostolic people led it to rediscover the pastoral genius of the patristic catechists of the fourth century and to enrich theology again with the living mystery of the Body of Christ.

Summing Up the Contribution

Liégé was not alone in this breakthrough in pastoral education and practical theology. His colleagues at the Institut Catholique, especially his student Jacques Audinet who came to be well known in the United States, were important pioneers with him. However, some commentators consider Liégé the most important figure in the renaissance of French pastoral theology both because of his keen mind and his important leadership.[40]

What did he actually accomplish?[41] In his writings on catechetics and the spiritual life Liégé was a popularising theologian who aimed to communicate with a broad spectrum of readers. He never got around to writing his *magnum opus*. Instead, he wrote critically important essays on faith, theological method, catechesis, and ministry for the encyclopedia *Catholicisme*; a great number of book chapters treating these same topics, and hundreds of essays on pastoral life and ministry for the journals *Parole et Mission* and *Équipes Enseignantes*. Two of his books on catechesis were translated into English, *Consider Christian Maturity* and *What is Christian Life?* In addition, he wrote introductory prefaces for works that ended up being landmarks in the development of French pastoral theology.[42]

Liégé knew how people often find themselves in spots where they are unexpectedly vulnerable to the redeeming power of the gospel. As a catechist, he was aware that he would sustain the interest of individuals only by transforming congregations into living communities of Christian

---

40. This includes Bradbury himself who also cites in this sense Marcel Viau, *Introduction aux études pastorales* (Montréal: Mediaspaul, 1987), and G Adler and G Vogeleisen, *Un siècle de catéchèse en France 1893-1980* (Paris: Beauchesne, 1981).
41. Bradbury provides a rich summary of Liégé's lifetime of achievements in his Part Four, *The Pastoral Theology of Pierre-André Liégé*, especially 181f.
42. Nicholas Bradbury includes a bibliography of Liégé's published works in his dissertation (*The Pastoral Theology of Pierre-André Liégé*).

friendship. Well before Vatican II, Liégé was convinced that the *people of God* was the fundamental category for the church. This was a rock solid biblical intuition that grew consistently in his life and work.

As a pastoral theologian Liégé was interested in not only priestly formation, but lay leadership as well. His idea of the church was thoroughly missionary and he imagined an evangelizing role for every one of the faithful. As a systematic theologian, Liégé attempted to describe the content and method of an effective pastoral theology. He drew upon psychology, sociology, and other human sciences to clarify the tasks of pastoral ministry. He was particularly sensitive to developmental psychology and the implications of human development for preaching and pastoral communication. In addition, especially through *Parole et Mission*, the pastoral journal for which he wrote regularly for two decades, Liégé tracked the new challenges for pastoral life and described the best options for responding to them.

Jean-Pierre Jossua has written about the daunting multiplicity of activities that Liégé became involved in. In the midst of juggling commitments to bishops, academics, and lay leaders, he managed somehow to make them all feel that he was completely present to them. He pushed himself to the limit, slept very little (in general without going to bed), and remained dynamic all the same. In addition, he never lost his interest in young people and found time to take care of adolescents in trouble. Further he managed "to be a confessor to duchesses (arousing the jealousy of some of the priests in his aristocratic priory); to vote socialist (he was a priest! as a young bourgeois I never got over it), and still to be a confidant of several cardinals."[43]

This zealous priest who was so engaged in others' needs and concerns maintained his theological and professional integrity. No one ever complained that he let his study, his teaching, his administrative work, or his writing slip. Regrets came later, when colleagues lamented that he never found the time to write the great book he always wanted to write, an introduction to pastoral theology that would synthesise what he had done over thirty years.[44]

---

43. Jossua, 'Une foi de chair et de sang', in *PAL*, 26.
44. Personally I have often thought it a shame that no one has created a 'Liégé Reader' by culling key articles from *Parole et Mission* and elsewhere that demonstrate Liégé's leading intuitions and summarise his achievements. His principal concerns and pastoral intuitions are as valuable today as they were thirty years ago. Perhaps someday that will

Despite his administrative and pastoral responsibilities, he made his mark on the church. He was treasured by his Dominican colleagues, his co-workers, his students, his bishop friends, and those who read him and heard his lectures. Yves Congar, in paying his friend this tribute shortly after his death, articulated what others felt: '[Père Liégé] was completely in control of his life, and with a willing gift of himself that showed no effort, he gave himself completely to the service of the gospel that was the love of his life. For me, he was the number one friar preacher—an unequaled living ideal.'[45]

---

happen.
45. Congar, 'Un idéal vivant inégalable' in *PAL*, 23.

Chapter 7

Marie-Alain Couturier: Ministry and the Arts

The twentieth century was a period of modernity in which science, art, psychology, and theater assumed new forms. The decades preceding and following the event of the Ecumenical Council Vatican II promoted various conversations between Roman Catholicism and modernity. Beyond the systems of Kant and Hegel and the psychologies of Nietzsche and Freud, from 1750 to 1950 science, theater, music, and art unfolded new cultural forms. The Vatican hierarchy bore a long-term hostility toward the modern world during the nineteenth and twentieth centuries. Should not the Gospel reject democracy, psychoanalysis, and abstract art? Fortunately, in France during the twentieth century there was a mature exploration, usage, and critique of modernity by Catholic intellectuals. Philosophers and theologians, writers and artists freed themselves from an anxiety about their own age and from excessive obedience to myopic church administrators. They sought out conversations with the worlds of self, freedom, and history. The Roman Catholic mentality celebrates the visual: a wide sacramentality continues the incarnation in architecture and sculpture, in liturgy and ritual.

Art and religion in the past century and a half could not avoid each other and inevitably they engaged in a dialogue between Christianity and the dynamics of modernity.[1] French Dominican friar Marie-Alain Couturier pursued a mission to understand religion in relationship to art, particularly Christianity and modern art. He appreciated new styles even as he recognised the traditions of great art in the past. He was able to see the

---

1. Couturier quotes André Malraux: 'Art is for modern artists the successor of the absolute. It is not a religion but it is a faith. It is not a ritual but it is the negation of an impure world' (*La vérité blessée* [Paris: Plon, 1984] 158).

spiritual in modern art and to criticise courageously bad art, old and new. Around the world his influence was considerable, in theory and in works of art.

At the end of the nineteenth century, with the work of Cézanne and Monet scarcely absorbed, a few young artists in France were pondering the sad, derivative state of religious art. The French philosopher Joseph Pichard organised conferences to discuss form and deformity in religious art. He also founded a periodical that would exert considerable influence: *L'Art Sacré Moderne.*[2] Its pages chronicled the atmosphere emerging from 1890 to 1914 and its critique and vision were taken up again after World War I. Pichard fostered the first attempts at a modern church architecture in Europe. Eighteen months after its inception, the journal *L'Art Sacré Moderne* was taken over by the publishing house of Éditions du Cerf which confided its direction to two Dominicans, P-R Régamey and Marie-Alain Couturier. They directed it from 1936 until 1954. Those two Dominicans were to play a central role in the dialogue between Roman Catholicism and modern art. Régamey's ideas became known in the English-speaking world through translations of *Religious Art in the Twentieth Century.*[3]

Couturier's Development as an Artist

Pierre Couturier was born in the region of the Loire on November 15, 1897 and was attracted to painting from his youth. He was mobilised for the First World War and wounded on the front in 1917.[4] The next year, he

2. (Paris: Arthaud, 1953), 21–43.
3. (Paris: Cerf, 1952); *Religious Art in the 20th Century* (New York: Herder, 1963) including chapters like 'The Laws of the Church', and 'The Non-Christian Artist in the Service of the Church', incorporating material from his earlier articles in *La Vie intellectuelle*. Régamey also wrote a pioneering book in the area of peace: *Non-Violence and the Christian Conscience* (New York: Herder and Herder, 1966).
4. See Sabine de Lavergne, *Art sacré et modernité: Les grandes années de la revue 'L'Art Sacré'* (Namur: Culture et Vérité, 1992); Françoise Caussé, 'Les Rapports des Dominicains avec L'Art sacré'; Saverio Xeres, *Architecture et vie dominicaine au XXe siècle* (Paris: Cerf, 2000), 169–76; Joanna Weber, *Couturier's Vision* (New Haven: Yale University Press, 1989); John Dillenberger, 'Artists and Church Commissions: Rubin's *The Church at Assy* Revisited', in Diane Apostolos-Cappadona, editor, *Art, Creativity, and the Sacred* (New York: Crossroad, 1983), 193–204. In 2004, to commemorate the fiftieth anniversary of the death of Couturier there was a conference in Nice to draw together the work of researchers who have explored his life and achievements: Antoine Lion, editor, *Marie-Alain Couturier (1897–1954): Un combat pour l'Art sacré: Mémoire Dominicaine VI* (Paris: Cerf, 2005) with a bibliography, hereafter cited as *Mém Dom VI.*

returned to painting, studied in Paris at the Académie de la Grande Chaumière, and had a show of watercolors. In 1919 he was painting in Paris with a group centered around Maurice Denis. He worked for the next five years in various churches in the media of fresco and stained glass, and with Denis he was responsible for the first church window of abstract art installed in a church at Le Raincy built in 1923.

During the early 1920s he toured Italy, read Paul Claudel, and met Jean Cocteau at the house of Jacques and Raïssa Maritain. He made the acquaintance of Henri Matisse, Pablo Picasso, and Le Corbusier. His odyssey moved within the psychology of faith as well as in the galleries of art. It drew him to religious life: first as a Benedictine oblate and then as a Dominican friar. Receiving the habit (and the name Marie-Alain) in 1925, he spoke of that day 'when freedom entered into my life, having the face of love.'[5] In the years immediately before and after his ordination in 1930, Couturier's superiors, far from discouraging his past interest and work in art, offered some commissions for frescoes: for instance, the chapel of the Dominicans at Oslo, Norway, and the private chapel of the Master General of the Dominicans at Santa Sabina in Rome. His style was figurative in a luminous, pastel manner, combining an impressionist approach with something of a pre-Raphaelite manner. Although his own work was not deeply modern it led him to appreciate new directions. 'By 1935, Couturier had become vocal in denouncing the state of the arts in the Church. He resented the Church's indifference towards the quality of its visual material and architecture.'[6]

Assigned to a priory in Paris while working on churches and windows up through 1937, Couturier was also active in a ministry of preaching and spiritual direction as well as in editing *L'Art Sacré*. Early in 1940, he arrived in New York to preach in French a series of Lenten Conferences at a parish in Manhattan and to lecture in Canada. The war trapped him in North America. He taught in French Canada, met artists in New York City, and served as a chaplain for French pilots in training in Jacksonville, Florida. He painted scenes for a Way of the Cross in the motherhouse of the Dominican Sisters at Elkins Park, Pennsylvania. 'His time in the United States and Canada proved to be a watershed for his thinking on the rela-

---

5. *L'Art sacré/Marie-Alain Couturier: textes choisis par Dominique de Ménil et Pie Duployé* (Houston: Menil Foundation/Hercher, 1983), 14; see Joël Boudaroua, 'Couturier, le dominicain', in *Mém Dom VI*, 31-42.
6. Weber, *Couturier's Vision*, 4.

tionship of abstraction and the sacred. This reevaluation was due in part to his involvement with New York's expatriate community. Couturier met Salvador Dali and developed a close friendship with the artist Fernand Léger and the writer Julien Green.[7] In 1942 Simone Weil at the suggestion of Jacques Maritain addressed her *Letter to a Religious* to Couturier when Weil and Couturier were in the United States.

Couturier returned to France in August 1945, deepened by his exile and filled with new ideas about art and faith. The church in its decoration and liturgy should relate positively and fearlessly to modern painting, sculpture, and architecture. The ultimate issue—beyond the modern lines of architecture or the new colored forms of Nolde, Rouault, and Chagall—was abstract art. Couturier appreciated the variety within contemporary art. Could not even abstract expressionism—that ultimate form of modernity—be contemplated without contempt? Writing on the spiritual dimension in abstract art, the Dominican found in music an interesting argument for non-figurative art. In a sense music was art without pictures, and like music abstract art was capable of being religious.

> Music proves that an abstract art form, that is, non-representational art, can have religious value. This therefore implies that an explicit reference to the order of sacred realities is not necessary; that the religious values, the religious or profane character of a work stems from the work itself, from its substantial elements. In music, this is true for the quality of sounds and rhythms. Why could it not be true for colors and lines in paintings?[8]

Abstract art was not necessarily atheistic or nihilistic. Line, form, and color inevitably reveal the spiritual. Is not modern art a kind of sacrament of the twentieth century?

The Divorce of Church from Culture

After 1870, the rapid de-Christianisation of Europe and the retreat of the church to the edge of culture had nourished fear and ignorance amid believers. In areas of culture, modernity developed independently of the ec-

---

7.   Weber, *Couturier's Vision*, 5.
8.   Couturier, 'Notes sur l'Abstraction', in *Art et Liberté* (Paris: Cerf, 1957), 43.

clesiastical world. 'What are the reasons for this?' Couturier asked. An immobility nourished by much of the ecclesiastical milieu of the nineteenth century clung to the older academic art and avoided the mentality and style of recent artists. French Catholicism was marginalised at the time of Proust, Debussy, and Monet. That social isolationism was furthered by what Couturier called the 'Byzantinism' of Catholic hierarchical circles in Italy and Spain, an ecclesiology aiming at a control of doctrine and at a feudal religious involvement in politics.[9] The long dialogue between the sacred and the arts that sustained the cultures of the Middle Ages, the Renaissance, and the Baroque had faded. After the early nineteenth century, the church turned to mediocre talents, to merchants and carpenters of an art and architecture that seemed religious because it presented images of Christian figures caught up in intense emotion. If the church continued the cultural diaspora it had nurtured since King Louis XVI and Pope Gregory XVI, from 1850 to 1950, the world of Catholics would become a ghetto. 'Ultimately nothing is more opposed to the Gospel than the mentality of the ghetto or the sect.'[10]

The large basilicas at Lourdes, Lyons-Fourvière, and Lisieux were constructs of an art that was imitative, mediocre, and even confused. Those churches were gigantic but without mystical depth. Displaying the same superficiality were the almost hundred churches built in recent decades in the environs of Paris without the advice of a single significant architect. Couturier often cited André Malraux in *L'Art Sacré* with whose breadth of vision he had much in common. Both agreed that there was a misunderstanding of what beauty and objectivity now were.

Championing Modern Religious Art

There was also the widespread rejection of any contact with modern artists because they were not believers. The church had to rethink and restate its ideas and goals for ecclesiastical art. To appreciate the problem which Couturier and Régamey faced is to ponder the division between a representational art—in the style of a nineteenth-century version of the Baroque—and a modern art.[11] The church should step back and let the free

---

9. '"The great scandal of the nineteenth century", said Pius XI, "is that the church has lost the working class." Not only the working class but philosophers, poets, and artists' (Couturier *La vérité blessée*, 27).
10. Couturier, *L'Art sacré: Textes choisis,* 144.
11. 'It is necessary to be against the Baroque and not be seduced by it. The Baroque has

genius of the artist provide 'the elaboration of forms, their birth which occurs in liberty, purity, and weakness aided by friendship, respect, and prayer.'[12] The artist may live independent of Christian faith, and yet still own mysterious lines to the transcendent and the mystical. The introduction of Christianity to the varieties of modern art—something quite difficult—would be for Couturier no less than 'the rebirth of Christian art . . . the reform of ideas, the restoration of visual sensitivity.'[13] Purification and liberation mark that move from an exact image to the variety and depth of beauty in form. In a great work of art a harmony of lines and colors can give in their formal accord an overall impact. Beauty lives free from academic imperialism, traditional ossification, and bourgeois conformism. It also escapes theological immaturity.

In the striking black and white illustrations of *L'Art Sacré* a Romanesque church, a pagan temple, an American dam, an African village show a formal dynamism and spiritual depth. They all display 'the multiple and living beauty of being . . . images taken from natural realities and even from industry, recalling that admirable forms are born without any need of art but through the rigor of mathematics or by means of a healthy conception of function and goal.'[14] *L'Art Sacré* observed that in regions at that time designated by the church as 'mission fields' the problems of art and sacramentality were compounded, since the church understood neither contemporary art nor the modernity of the traditional art of Africa and Asia. Everywhere Catholicism must adjust itself to a new relationship between the profane and the sacred.

Church leadership, however, did little: it was unwilling to support any form of modern art. In France after World War II it was clear to Couturier that minor talents would not be able to fashion religious art through modern forms. He conceived the idea of involving the great figures of modern art in providing art for the churches. Could not artists alienated from or indifferent to the church paint the spiritual in color and line? For authentic Christian art to exist, each generation must appeal to the masters of

---

a worldly spirit: the naked angels, the virtues that are half naked women . . . Baroque sentimentality is interested in those aspects of the saints that are the last to be purified or, perhaps, those aspects that express a kind of revenge through sensuality' (*La vérité blessée*, 230).

12. Couturier, *L'Art sacré: Textes choisis*, 36.

13. Couturier, *L'Art sacré: Textes choisis*, 14. This project was being pursued during this period in North America by figures like Paul Tillich and Maurice Lavanoux.

14. Couturier, *L'Art sacré: Textes choisis*, 17.

living art, and today those masters come first from secular art. Who today is commissioning art for churches from contemporary ateliers? This is not a question of spotlighting the sensational but of searching out individuals in whom in contemporary times (no other times exist) art is alive. One employs life and art where one finds them. As his own work as an artist became less and less important, Couturier brought his ideas to realization through active friendships with artists and cultural innovators of his day. Régamey wrote: 'From the time of his training at the Ateliers d'Art Sacré under Denis and Desvallières, Père Couturier's greatest ambition was to revive Christian art by appealing to the independent masters of his time.'[15]

L'Art Sacré became linked with the Centre de Pastorale Liturgique in Paris and took on a focus of visual catechesis for the church in France. Couturier and Régamey thought of their writing as an apostolate. Françoise Caussé observes that *L'Art Sacré* became simultaneously a publication on spirituality as well as on the arts.[16] The Jesuit exegete Pierre Gibert recalls how important *L'Art Sacré* was for him in the 1950s. The French church was reeling from the impact of Godin's book, *France, Pays de Mission*, and young priests and seminarians were looking for signs of hope and renewal. *L'Art Sacré* was that kind of sign, carrying the message that the old statuary and sentimental images in the Saint Sulpice style were lethal to a living spirituality; it gave concrete examples of how to live the faith in an environment of beauty.[17]

Couturier became a missionary of a message of liberation from religious sentimentality and of the purification of sacramental sensibilities; he visited parishes and their pastors and congregations. He was responsible for linking local churches with gifted artists and architects and encouraging communities to give a practical reality to purification and liberation as older, even historical parish churches were renovated or new churches were planned. In the surrounding areas clergy and people saw these changes in the parish church.

The outreach of *L'Art Sacré* moved beyond France. In the United States, as well as in Germany in other parts of Europe, priests, religious, and seminarians looked for the appearance of the next number of the journal. For them Couturier was a sort of compass pointing the way to integrity.

15. *Religious Art in the Twentieth Century*, 236.
16. Caussé, 'De la possibilité d'un art sacré contemporain: à travers la correspondence Couturier/Régamey', in *Mém Dom VI*, 125–50.
17. Gibert, 'L'injustice de l'échec, ou: le P Couturier a-t-il été vaincu', in *Mém Dom VI*, 153–61.

A Breakthrough in Church Art

A diocesan priest Abbé Devémy, chaplain at a sanatorium at Assy opposite Mont Blanc, thought of commissioning artists who were not 'third-rate' for a church in that area near the Alps, a church to serve sanatorium patients and their visitors. He discussed the project between 1932 and 1935 with Couturier. In 1939 Couturier stopped to visit his friend and was asked to collaborate in planning the church of 'Our Lady of All Graces'. The project began by acquiring a window designed by Rouault. The war years intervened and then came conversations with Léger and Chagall on the prospect of their collaboration at Assy.[18] In a decisive move, Couturier attracted for the decoration of the new church not only Léger, Chagall, and Rouault but Braque, Matisse, and Lipchitz. Assy was consecrated in June, 1950.

Devémy, the pastor of Assy, observed that Assy is not a masterpiece—it lacks rigor in organisation—but is a cultural-theological statement of the greatest import.[19] The tapestry backdrop for the sanctuary was done by Jean Lurçat, the facade mosaic by Léger, the tabernacle door by Braque, windows by Rouault, and stained glass and a ceramic mural by Chagall.[20] What, Couturier asked, is the lesson of the Assy church? 'This will touch so many in so many places where the news of it reaches them: modern art's overflowing, violent and madly generous life was to be accepted, blessed by the holy, ancient, and maternal Church. Offered to Christ as the greatest tribute. This is Assy's real lesson, its only lesson.'[21]

Assy did attract enormous attention: in the United States *Life* magazine featured it. Reactionary Catholics, however, looked with fear at contacts between art and religion. Their attacks usually focused upon the lack of a traditional religious figure even if the works of art at Assy were in fact not fully abstract. Furthermore, in the view of the reactionaries were these

---

18. For a history of the genesis of Assy and for a detailed study of its works of art, see W. Rubin, 'Decadence and the Dominicans', in *Modern Sacred Art and the Church of Assy* (New York: Columbia University Press, 1961); John Dillenberger, 'Artists and Church Commissions: Rubin's *The Church at Assy* Revisited', 193–99.
19. Couturier, *L'Art sacré: Textes choisis*, 52, 56.
20. For a list of the works of art see John Dillenberger, 'Artists and Church Commissions: Rubin's *The Church at Assy* Revisited', 76–77. On Rouault see Stephen Schloesser, *Jazz Age Catholicism: Mystic Modernism in Postwar Paris 1919-1933* (Toronto: University of Toronto Press, 2005), 213-244; *Mystic Masque: Semblance and Reality in Georges Rouault 1871-1958* (Chicago: University of Chicago Press, 2008).
21. Couturier, *L'Art sacré*, Assy 1–2 (1950), 16–17.

forms not only strange but empty and ugly? Conservative reactions became vocal both in France and in Rome. Realisations of modern freedom and subjectivity were offensive as was the lack of faith or ecclesial membership of the artists. In the following years, Régamey and Couturier worked on a dual front: explaining and encouraging the breakthrough of twentieth century art in the decoration of Assy, Vence, and Audincourt, and defending the very possibility of this new religious art to the *intégristes* and to Rome.

Pius XII's encyclical *Mediator Dei* from 1947 and his allocution in 1950 on sacred art were positive:

> The function of all art lies in fact in breaking through the narrow and tortuous enclosure of the finite in which man is immersed while living here below and in providing a window on the infinite for his hungry soul . . . Naturally, we are far from thinking that in order to be interpreters of God in the sense just mentioned, artists must treat explicity religious subjects . . . Do not vainly try to give the human without the divine, nor nature without its Creator. Harmonize the finite with the infinite, the temporal with the eternal, man with God.[22]

That irenic approach, however, was not maintained in an 'Instruction' issued not by the Pope but by Vatican officials in June, 1952. That text, after listing the censures of Nicaea and Trent against distortion and innovation in art, emphasised the link between sacred art and liturgy. If it deplored mediocre, mass-produced images and praised artists who are outstanding for their technique, it discouraged 'unusual images . . . not in conformity with the approved usage of the church.'[23] Apparently new art expressed not only the much deplored abstractness but could express false dogma and be the occasion of dangerous error. There was no mention that most traditional religious art was photographic and theologically shallow.

By 1953 and 1954 the controversy over sacred art had become one facet of a spreading crisis in the Catholic Church. Contemporary theo-

---

22. Pius XII, 'Function of Art', in *The Catholic Mind* 50 (1952): 697–68.
23. '*Instructio . . "De Arte Sacra"*' (from the Suprema Sacra Congregatio S. Officii) *Acta Apostolicae Sedis*, 44 (1952): 542–545; (English translation: 'On Sacred Art', in *Catholic Mind* 50 [1952]: 699–702).

logical directions had been summarily dismissed in 1950 by Pius XII's encyclical *Humani Generis*. The priest-workers were ordered to take no new recruits, and participation in the liturgy by the baptised was ended. Now theological contacts with culture were to be ended. Emmanuel Suarez, the superior general of the Dominicans, came from Rome to Paris (at the insistence of the Vatican) to remove from their positions the French provincials and to cut off prominent theologians like Yves Congar from their professorships. He also removed the director of the Éditions du Cerf publishing house where *L'Art Sacré* was edited. From the mid-1950s, until John XXIII announced a new ecumenical council in 1959, the renewal of the Catholic Church in the laboratory of France came largely to a halt. Couturier wrote:

> More and more I see the church as a large mutilated tree, a large trunk which has some beautiful branches but there are also branches dry and dead . . . The Latin church is still catholic in legal assertion but not in fact. Successive crises have fashioned in Rome complexes of fear, defense mechanisms responding to serious problems with suspicions of heresy and condemnation.[24]

Despite difficulties Assy led to similar projects. The Church of the Sacred Heart at Audincourt had stained glass by Léger and mosaics by Jean Bazaine. A Dominican sister at a cloister in Vence near Nice asked Henri Matisse if he would consider designing their new chapel. Couturier and a young Dominican, L-B Rayssiguier, were soon brought in to offer advice on the project and they worked with Matisse on the design and the decorations for the chapel.[25] Matisse's windows, vestments, and painted figures were widely recognised as a new direction in Christian art. After the chapel was dedicated in summer of 1951, Couturier recalled: 'Chagall after his visit to Vence said to me: "This is something new—that an artist

24. *La vérité blessée*, 245.
25. See Henri Matisse, M-A Couturier, L-B Rayssiguier, *The Vence Chapel: The Archive of a Creation* (Houston: The Menil Foundation, 1999); this book through entries from Couturier's diaries presents a portrait of the personality, theology, and spirituality of Matisse. And Marc Chauveau, 'Vence: Matisse et Couturier, quatre années de connivance', in *Mém Dom VI*, 107–25.

creating religious art has been chosen to make certain objects in this or that way."[26]

The famous architect Le Corbusier was planning a church in the same diocese as the church of Audincourt, a soaring ensemble of lines and glass and concrete in the countryside at Ronchamp. After his return from America, Couturier became familiar with Le Corbusier and discussed projects with him.[27] The Dominicans of the Lyons Province engaged Le Corbusier in 1952 to build a house of studies in the hills outside Lyons, La Tourette. 'In discussing the monastery with Le Corbusier, Couturier had suggested that he visit the Cistercian monastery, Le Thoronet. He felt that this twelfth century monastery captured the essence of monastic life. In their correspondence, Couturier explained the rules by which the Dominicans live and even suggested some plans for the new priory of La Tourette.'[28] Its construction was complete in 1959.

Couturier's health began to deteriorate in 1953, and following surgery in that year he never fully recovered his health. He died (without seeing Ronchamp or La Tourette completed) on the 9th of February 1954. Great architectural spaces of worship and transcendence were the result of Couturier's mission to let modern art express the sacred in line and color. The outcome emerges in what might be called the religious art gallery of Assy, the windows and mosaic by Léger and Bazaine at Audincourt, Matisse's chapel for the Dominican sisters at Vence, and the Dominican priory for study, La Tourette.

Couturier did not live to see the flourishing dialogue between art and faith and the triumph of his ideas in France and around the world. During the years following World War II he brought a new vision to the church. Father Régamey, his colleague in this endeavor, often referred to these years as 'a springtime without a summer'.[29] Couturier hoped that the church would speak once again in the language of the world. His struggle had not been an easy one: in his last years, he came under severe attack by Rome. Anticipating Vatican II, he consistently emphasised the incarnational nature of Christianity, observing how the Holy Spirit refuses to

---

26. *La vérité blessée*, 245.
27. Valerio Casali, 'Marie-Alain Couturier et Le Corbusier', in *Mém Dom VI*, 87–126.
28. Weber, *Couturier's Vision*, 10-11; see Anton Henze, Bernhard Moosbrugger, *La Tourette: The Le Corbusier Monastery* (London: Lund Humphries, 1966).
29. Régamey, 'Introduction', to Couturier, *L'Évangile est à l'extrême* (Paris: Cerf, 1970), 8.

be limited by encrusted traditions.[30] Couturier's work sought to liberate people so that they might see the present and the future in art and visual sacraments. His apostolate was for the future, and his perspective was universal.

John Dillenberger has shown how this movement influenced Protestant churches in the United States like St Peter's Lutheran Church in New York City.[31] John and Dominique de Menil commissioned a chapel in Houston for meditation, a plain interior whose walls held large paintings by Mark Rothko. At the outside entrance there is a pool and a sculpture by Barnett Newman. The chapel was conceived as a place of holy quiet in the midst of the upheavals of the 1960s. John de Menil's brother was a Dominican in the same Province as Couturier. Calvin Tomkins wrote in *The New Yorker*:

> The Rothko Chapel [was] inspired by Father Couturier's efforts to renew the sources of sacred art, and by their own conviction that 'modern churches' as Dominique expressed it 'are too damn awful.' The de Menils had commissioned Rothko in 1964 to do a series of murals for a Catholic chapel that Philip Johnson was originally going to build on the St. Thomas campus. Inside the octagonal brick structure, which opened in 1971 . . . Rothko's fourteen monumental abstract paintings resonate in silence, their dark colors—black, deep maroon, and raw umber, with tinges of blue—interacting and filling the space . . . Opposite the chapel stands Newman's 'Broken Obelisk,' which the de Menils had tried to give to the city of Houston. It is the chapel's vital counterpart and antithesis—a great sculptural expression for the age of doubt.[32]

---

30. 'I believe that the influence of Couturier and Régamey has been considerable. They were cultural and spiritual pioneers of Vatican II's document on the church in the modern world. This has brought a considerable conversion among church leaders, bishops and laity and has led to a better development of the gifts of nature and grace. It is useless to speak of religious art without speaking of art' (Thomas Patfoort, 'Quelques souvenirs de vie commune', in *Mém Dom VI*, 63).

31. J Dillenberger, 'Artists and Church Commissions: Rubin's *The Church at Assy* Revisited', 193–97.

32. Calvin Tomkins, 'The Benefactor', in *The New Yorker* (June 8, 1998), 62; *Art and Activism. Projects of John and Dominique de Menil* (Houston: The Menil Collection, 2010); Pamela Smart, *Sacred Modern: Faith, Activism and Aesthetics in The Menil Collection*

Dominique de Menil recalled:

> I would like to recall two events which occurred before and
> after the war. The influence they had on us was decisive.
> In January of 1936, Father Congar delivered eight lectures
> on ecumenism that marked the beginning of his ecumeni-
> cal career. I had the privilege to hear him and it marked me
> for life. In the summer of 1952 we visited with Father Cou-
> turier, another Dominican, the churches where Léger and
> Matisse, two towering artists of their time, had contributed
> their greatest work. We visited also the site where Le Cor-
> busier was going to build his famous chapel at Ronchamp.
> We saw what a master could do for a religious building when
> he is given a free hand. He can exalt and uplift as no one else.
> The influence of those events was lasting. If we played a part
> in the birth of this Chapel, which indeed we did, it stems
> from the orientation we received in those early days, through
> those two men.[33]

Couturier's stimulus to the dialogue between Christianity and modern art
inspired a second building in Houston: a museum for The Menil Collection in 1987.

In the 1980s Dominique de Menil decided to introduce Couturier
anew by publishing a selection of passages from *L'Art Sacré* and from his
notes and journals. *L'Art Sacré: Textes Choisis* presents excerpts from the
periodical as it touches on art in Africa and poor French neighborhoods,
on implicitly sacred art, and on Vence and Audincourt, material from
1939 to 1953.[34] Striking black and white photographs illustrate the texts.

The Dominican had published a few books and articles, occasional
pieces that were insightful.[35] His book *Art et Catholicisme* from 1941 held

---

(Austin: University of Texas Press, 2010).

33. Dominique de Menil, *Address at the Opening of the Rothko Chapel,* 27th of February
1971; see Susan J Barnes, *The Rothko Chapel* (Austin: University of Texas Press, 1989).
Jane Owen, restorer of New Harmony, Indiana, wrote that Couturier was the 'first
colossus' who stood astride the Catholic Church and modern art. Jacques Lipchitz, the
sculptor, and Paul Tillich, the theologian, were the second and third (William R Crout,
'Jane Blaffer Owen: A Personal Tribute', in *Bulletin of the North American Paul Tillich
Society* 36/3 [2010]: 3).

34. *L'Art sacré: Textes choisis* (Houston: Menil Foundation/Hercher, 1983).

35. *Art et Catholicisme* (Montreal: Editions de l'Arbre, 1941) and *Chroniques* (Montreal:

chapters on markers along the 'royal road of art' like El Greco and Picasso, and then considered Christian art and Catholicism, and sacred art in Canada. He composed studies on Léger and on the architect Marcel Parizeau.[36] A second book *La Vérité Blessée*, drawing on the provincial archives of the Paris Province of Dominicans and the MA Couturier Archives created by The Menil Foundation in 1975,[37] assembles selections from journals and essays, and from sketches for articles and talks not published. There is a forward by the French philosopher of science and art Michel Serres.[38] Couturier's spiritual life is glimpsed through his observations on or quotations from literary figures. Paragraphs depict conversations at meetings with figures from the arts, while longer segments give descriptions of art, the sacred, and the sacramental. 'I believe in the continuity of the life of forms, in the homogeneity of their evolution, and yet it is true that the appearance of a genius is unforeseeable, and that such an appearance calls everything into question, reversing the course of life, orienting everything to the new genius.'[39] Dominique de Menil in her introduction to this book writes that 'it is not a question of re-introducing someone forgotten but of receiving his presence anew'. This is the presence of someone who broke through into unexplored frontiers, someone who, when modern art was dismissed as secular, atheist or neurotic, became the friend of Braque, Matisse, and Picasso.[40] The excerpts from the journals and addresses in *La Vérité Blessée* are sources for learning about Couturier's life and work, while the pages reproduced from *L'Art Sacré* touch on the problematic of relating Christianity, seemingly so explicit in its religious objects, to an art increasingly abstract and transcendental. In the pages of both books we hear the voice of an original thinker, a contemplative priest who converses with the great figures of the French cultural world after 1900. 'The sacred is not a grand spectacle but a living communion.'[41]

Éditions de l'Arbre, 1947) were brought together in the posthumous *Art et liberté spiri-tuelle* (Paris: Cerf, 1958). After Couturier's death Régamey published *Discours de mariage—garder libre* translated into English as *Wedding Sermons* (London: Blackfriars, 1957).

36. *Fernand Léger: la forme humaine dans l'espace* (Montréal: Les Éditions de l'Arbre, 1945); *Marcel Parizeau, architecte* (Montréal: L'Arbre, 1945).

37. *La vérité blessée* (Paris: Cerf, 1984).

38. 'Note de l'éditeur', *La vérité blessée*, 13.

39. *La vérité blessée*, 147ff.

40. Dominique de Ménil, 'Pour laisser parler le Père Couturier', *L'Art Sacré: Textes choisis*, 9.

41. *La vérité blessée*, 317.

Couturier did not claim to have resolved the problems of style and spirit in modern art. He certainly altered the relationship between art and church in the twentieth century. Both theology and art had sunk into forms that were too cerebral, too literal, too superficial. He liberated religious art from past academic enclosures as his Dominican confreres were liberating theology from past neo-scholasticisms. The word 'living' occurs repeatedly in his writings. Only the living can flourish in the now. Modern art and the sacred, far from being esoteric hobbies, mirrored the problem of how Catholicism in its theology and life would express itself in the culture of the decades after 1900 and 1950. What the priest-workers articulated in the factories, what the theologians wrote in their books on the interplay of nature and grace in the individual, what the liturgists and musicians led in assemblies of the baptised, Couturier pursued in art.

The Church in History

All through the twentieth century, creative people led the Catholic Church in new directions. The church became both more biblical and more expressive of its ancient roots even as it became more modern and more in touch with the world around it. After centuries of defensive self-preoccupation, the Roman Catholic Church began to give birth to innovative thinkers whose instinct was not to condemn challenging developments in history, politics and the social sciences, but rather to consider, critique, and integrate them. Such innovations in Christian self-understanding, emerging at the end of the nineteenth century and during the first half of the twentieth, planted seeds that came to birth in the Second Vatican Council. But today the church finds itself on the fence, so to speak, between the authoritarianism and defensiveness of the nineteenth century, on the one hand, and the challenge to engage a world of instant communication, globalization and radical individualism, on the other. So positioned, it still has a lot to learn from those who worked tirelessly for ecclesial renewal in the twentieth century.

The seven theologians whose careers are discussed here exemplify the transition from a defensive premodern worldview to an open and engaged dialogue with the contemporary world. They restored to theology a sense of history and integrated into their theological method the contributions of modernity. They taught theologies from the early centuries to people living in the twentieth century and reframed contemporary Catholic theology and liturgy in the light of modern biblical scholarship. Above all, drawing from the Bible, they underlined the inescapable centrality of community for the faithful, each one of whom is endowed with an individual destiny. The Dominicans studied here are priests and theologians, but in each case they are connected to lay colleagues, to diocesan clergy, and to the renewal of pastoral life. It is no accident that they set the theme *the people of God* at the heart of their reflections. The church is not essentially the clergy—popes, bishops, and priests—but a people of all the baptised whose head is Christ. The fact that this perspective is being reclaimed by Catholics around the world is due in no small part to the revival of church life that ensued after World War II in France.

At home in the twentieth century, these Catholic theologians no longer wanted to be defined as separated from or hostile to the world around them. They felt obliged to pay attention to and dialogue with the human sciences in their treatment of religion. They knew that they had things to learn about the Christian life from those who did not share their faith—from historians, sociologists, psychoanalysts, and others. In a special way, they felt the need to respect historical scholarship as an awakening to inescapable facts. Their understanding both of the Bible and of the church was being enriched at the same time as it was being challenged by history. Unafraid, they learned and responded, and in doing so replanted the church's intellectual life in the context of their own time and circumstances.

What fashioned this gradual but influential movement? A church that had changed little since 1600 manifested signs of new life in the 1930s, underwent a creative climax in the 1950s, and expanded into the dramatic fruitfulness of the 1960s and after. At issue were new directions in liturgy, religious education, and theology that modified the life of the Christian churches in profound and lasting ways. In seeking a deeper and more authentic theology, these scholars discovered transforming resources in biblical studies and patristic sources. By doing so, they themselves became dialogue partners and peers of their colleagues in academia as well as leaders in retooling pastoral life and liturgy inside the church. They fulfilled the old dream of bringing science and theology into partnership in a prolific and productive way.

As a result, it became clear that the church had to be more than ecclesiastical authorities or a machinery of graces or a program of yearly festivals. The church's sacramental yeast was not closeted in dim churches, but active in people's lives. The world was not a quicksand of temptation and evil, but an environment of grace finding expression in both history and community. The paradigm for the efforts of these Dominicans is a pattern of concentric circles, of varied and wider circles of grace emanating from a center, Jesus and his Spirit. These concentric circles extend the reality of divine grace across different contexts: across the world of nonbelievers, across different rites and languages, across the structures of society, and across the pluralism of human religions.

For over a century, the French church had been weak and Catholics there had exercised very little influence in public life. A militant secularism (called in French the 'lay' spirit) had been dominant in political and academic circles. It aimed to make the public sphere completely free of religious influence. By the eighteenth century, the Enlightenment completely dominated the universities and the educated classes. Following the French Revolution, religion was merely tolerated by the government when it was not coarsely manipulated. Religious orders were expelled from the country or even suppressed. The majority of the population, especially in urban centers, fell away from the church. This explains the dramatic nature of the reintroduction of religious life into France in the mid-nineteenth century by the Dominican Lacordaire, who insisted upon both the human right to freely express his religious faith and the need for the church to build a community coherent with the revolutionary ideals of 'freedom, equality, and fraternity'. As we have shown, the spirit and ideals of the French Dominicans of the twentieth century derive in great part from Lacordaire and the model he established for ecclesial loyalty and popular honesty.

Their deep-seated confidence in the validity of the intellectual life gave these Dominicans self-assurance as liturgists, exegetes, and theologians. The central fact of Christ's incarnation opened for them countless relationships and conversations with the world into which Christ was born and with those who studied it, whatever their discipline. When *Gaudium et Spes* finally articulated their attitude, it spoke of a mutually enriching dialogue between the church and the world which benefits them both (*GS* 40). (This is just one example of how theological initiatives undertaken earlier in the century found their fulfillment in the documents of the council.) In the work of our seven Dominicans, as well as in the research and writing of other Catholic scholars, artists, theologians, preachers, and pastoral activists after World War II, there were a number of common characteristics. Here are five of them:

Liberation: They felt liberated from the tendency to identify Christian theology with neo-scholastic metaphysics; likewise they felt free from the need to identify the spiritual life uniquely with obedience to church authority. Studying the Bible and the theologians of the early church set the faithful free to see the gospel with new depth and to infuse new vibrancy into a corporate understanding of the liturgy, especially the Eucharist. They produced new translations and commentaries on the Hebrew and Christian Scriptures. They published new editions of the works of theologians from the second to the sixth centuries, not because they were old but because they offered refreshing and often deeply pertinent alternatives to a too abstract and philosophical theology that they often called 'Baroque'.

Synthesis: Most of these thinkers were active in more than one area. They allowed theology to lead them to modern art or to find interpretations of the gospel in economic analysis. They linked the history of the church's reflective life to evangelization; the texts of tradition found expression in modern thought-forms and practical circumstances. Congar summed this up by pointing out that the council's vision was resolutely the perspective of salvation history—history mindful of eschatology. The council has integrated the best biblical, patristic and theological studies of the thirty years that went before it. For these Dominicans, the council's documents were understood to be a new foundation for on-going theological work that will be attentive to the human situation of a rapidly changing world.

Realism: The human mind actively explores what is essential about the realities it experiences and makes judgments accordingly. Seminal ideas and insights are more valuable than axioms and timeless conclusions. Theologians, philosophers, and historians are meant to be realists. Thomas Aquinas, the mentor of all Dominicans, presented creation and revelation as realms of reality. He emphasised the structure of the human personality and explained grace as a life-principle coming from God dwelling within us. For him, Christian theology was about realism, not about an ideal or abstract world.

History: The great dynamic principle and rediscovery for Vatican II was history. The long history of theology, the liturgy, and the church puts in perspective the contributions of Thomas Aquinas, Martin Luther, and the Reformation, for example, by surrounding them with the context of their culture and their times. As Yves Congar put it:

> Everything is absolutely historical, including the person of Jesus Christ. The gospel is historical; Thomas Aquinas is historical; Pope Paul VI is historical. Historical, however, does not mean just that Jesus came at a certain point in time, but that we have to draw the consequences of this fact and in-

terpret him by the times in which he lived. He developed like every other man, his consciousness grew, his knowledge expanded.

Catholic theology, after avoiding history and culture for so long, found itself in the twentieth century in the hands of scholars and ministers who rediscovered history as the gateway to theological depth and effective renewal.

Life in Today's Church: These theologians criticised the church as an ecclesiastical pyramid of baroque splendor isolated from society, and they offered instead ways to engage with the modern world. The renewal of biblical and theological studies that emerged was applied to the life of the church so as to render parish life vital and energising. Liturgy, with its sacraments for different moments in the life cycle, ecumenical dialogue between the divided branches of the church, the arts, and social concerns, all had a common focus on enhancing the life of grace in the faithful. This perspective led to a concern for adult faith formation, new forms of catechetical teaching, and a vision of the baptised faithful as agents of the church's proclamation of the kingdom of God.

The Dominicans were pioneers in critical movements with modest beginnings: Bible study groups, ecumenical institutes, informal groups of pastors, and spiritual formation for lay leaders. What was said of Chenu could be said of many of the others: 'Chenu was a man of the people, in both a sociological and theological sense. He was a man of the people and a theologian of the people of God . . . ' St Paul understood the church as continuing the heritage of Israel—a priestly people, a prophetic presence in the world.

There were other gifted Dominicans who were leaders in important areas of Catholic theology and culture. In publishing, there was M-D Bernadot who founded the innovative journal *Sept* in 1934. *Sept* undertook to follow political events in France and interpret them to the faithful. However, on the 27th of August 1937, *Sept* had to cease publication because of an intervention from Rome. The journal was suppressed by the Dominican Master General M-S Gillet, who was forced to act by order of the Vatican's Holy Office. The French Dominicans also founded the scholarly journal *Revue des Sciences Philosophiques et Théologiques* that disseminated the theological ideas of the French Dominicans. At a more pastoral and popular level, they founded as well the influential *La Vie Intellectuelle*, directed by Augustin Maydieu, and then later *La Vie Spirituelle*—both publications which attracted the attention of French intellectuals and pastoral leaders alike.

In philosophy, there were figures like M-D Roland-Gosselin and Dominique Dubarle; in ecumenism, Christophe Dumont who founded the Istina Center to advance dialogue with Russian and Slavic Christianity (it had a specialised library of 80,000 books and a journal with the same name as the center). In the arts, there were figures like Pie Régamey writing on art and peace and Raymond Bruckberger writing novels and cultural monographs and collaborating with Francis Poulenc as the librettist for his *Dialogue of the Carmelites*. In psychology, there was Albert Plé who brought Freud into dialogue with Catholic pastoral thought, and a bit later Jacques Pohier, who carried on this same tradition of dialogue between moral theology and psychoanalysis.

In liturgy, A-M Roguet was one of the founders of the French national liturgical center (*Centre National de Pastoral Liturgique*) that became the clearing house for liturgical renewal up to the council and beyond. Roguet wrote a number of books on pastoral liturgy that guided the liturgical renewal through the 1940s and 50s, many of them translated into English. His younger confrere Pierre-Marie Gy was a widely read liturgical scholar who also created and directed the graduate program in liturgical studies (*Institut Supérieur de Pastorale Liturgique*) at the Institut Catholique in Paris. For two generations, he trained liturgical scholars and pastoral leaders from around the world. With great skill and discretion, Gy represented the concerns of French bishops and pastors to the Holy See and assisted in writing countless official documents to adjust general norms to the concrete pastoral situation of the French church.

For all these figures, the life of the church was not about recapturing a sacred past, but about incarnating a graced presence; not about nostalgia for a former perfection, but about hope for a future fullness. Vatican II transmitted many of the Dominicans' ideas and projects to the entire world. Without slighting the considerable contributions of Germany, Belgium, the Netherlands, Austria, and Switzerland, the claim can be made that the council was very much a gift of French theology. In the decades since the council, the church has in large part adopted a new orientation of embracing freedom of research, global human concerns, advocacy for human dignity and social justice, and interest in world religions. In the spirit of *Gaudium et Spes*, the postconciliar church is attentive to the possibility of a fuller incarnation of the mystery of Christ through its enculturation in all these dimensions. In the same spirit, it recognises its responsibility to constantly scan the signs of the times to maintain its grasp on the evolution of society.

Our seven French Dominicans were intellectuals in the sense of being people immersed in the world of learning, literature and the arts; they were all, in some sense, public intellectuals concerned to debate and influence public opinion and policy. They were profoundly engaged, first in the sense of personal commitment, but also in the sense of working toward clear goals for a purification and renewal of the church. What is so interesting about their stories is the diversity of projects and achievements that flowed out of individuals who all shared fundamentally the same sort of religious and intellectual formation. Some became renowned in theological research, others in preaching and pastoral leadership, others in social and economic justice, and still others in literature and the arts. They shared their stories with one another and supported one another across the boundaries of their divergent professions, a fraternal solidarity that was possible because ultimately they all saw themselves as serving the same cause. They all strove to render the church once again a fully apostolic expression of the Body of Christ alive and active in all its members.

Yves Congar described tradition as something more profound than dogmas or documents and more authoritative than precepts or decrees. Tradition is in the activity of the Holy Spirit in the church as the vivifying, animating principle of the Body of Christ. Through tradition, the Spirit touches everyone in the church, stimulating all to think and to act.

Perhaps this is the way to summarise the theme of attention to the signs of the times for our seven Dominicans. None of them was content to imagine the church as an institution fixed forever in laws and custom, to consider it a divine monarchy with a hierarchical bureaucracy, or to accept that its fundamental attitude has to be nostalgia for a perfect past. Motivated by intellectual honesty, theological rigor, pastoral compassion, and creative vision, they re-imagined the church according to the charter of the Scriptures and the ancient theology of the patristic age as a living spiritual organism embracing all the baptised as peers in the Body of Christ. They saw all the faithful as sharing a vocation to offer potent witness in society to the kingdom of God. Their challenging initiatives met with obstacles from ecclesiastical authorities haunted by an idealised past.

Their central insights were powerful. Sertillanges recognized that arid rationalism would no longer speak to the hearts of twentieth-century people. Chenu understood that Christian theology could flourish in the culture only as a message for the whole of humanity. Congar appreciated that the church had to understand and act as what it really is—a people of God alive in every part. Lebret saw that the economy had to be part of the church's pastoral concern, since it is there that human lives thrive or flounder. Loew understood that the world of workers was a spiritual universe that required authentic, sensitive pastoral attention. Liégé recognized that the twentieth century needed informed, creative, adult laity who could be evangelizers in the context of their professional milieu. Couturier envisaged a church where living art and Christian imagination would become mutually enhancing cultural partners. They read these signs and invented pastoral responses that still enliven our ecclesial life.

These French Dominicans faced the changes in the world about them and they read the hunger of their contemporaries for a fuller Christian life. Imagination and creativity led them to respond. Their stories still remain powerfully encouraging.

Indices

Index of Subjects

Index of Names

CPSIA information can be obtained
at www.ICGtesting.com
Printed in the USA
BVHW030549210721
611889BV00002B/106